Death--and After?

by Annie Besant

PREFACE.

Few words are needed in sending this little book out into the world. It is the third of a series of Manuals designed to meet the public demand for a simple exposition of Theosophical teachings. Some have complained that our literature is at once too abstruse, too technical, and too expensive for the ordinary reader, and it is our hope that the present series may succeed in supplying what is a very real want. Theosophy is not only for the learned; it is for all. Perhaps among those who in these little books catch their first glimpse of its teachings, there may be a few who will be led by them to penetrate more deeply into its philosophy, its science, and its religion, facing its abstruser problems with the student's zeal and the neophyte's ardour. But these Manuals are not written for the eager student, whom no initial difficulties can daunt; they are written for the busy men and women of the work-a-day world, and seek to make plain some of the great truths that render life easier to bear and death easier to face. Written by servants of the Masters who are the Elder Brothers of our race, they can have no other object than to serve our fellow-men._

DEATH--AND AFTER?

Who does not remember the story of the Christian missionary in Britain, sitting one evening in the vast hall of a Saxon king, surrounded by his thanes, having come thither to preach the gospel of his Master; and as he spoke of life and death and immortality, a bird flew in through an unglazed window, circled the hall in its flight, and flew out once more into the darkness of the night. The Christian priest bade the king see in the flight of the bird within the hall the transitory life of man, and claimed for his faith that it showed the soul, in passing from the hall of life, winging its way not into the darkness of night, but into the sunlit radiance of a more glorious world. Out of the darkness, through the open window of Birth, the life of a man comes to the earth; it dwells for a while before our eyes; into the darkness, through the open window of Death, it vanishes out of our sight. And man has questioned ever of Religion, Whence comes it? Whither goes it? and the answers have varied with the faiths. To-day, many a hundred year since Paulinus talked with Edwin, there are more people in Christendom who question whether man has a spirit to come anywhere or to go anywhither than, perhaps, in the world's history could ever before have been found at one time. And the very Christians who claim that Death's terrors have been abolished, have surrounded the bier and the tomb with more gloom and more dismal funeral pomp than have the votaries of any other creed. What can be more depressing than the darkness in which a house is kept shrouded, while the dead body is awaiting sepulture? What more repellent than the sweeping robes of lustreless crape, and the purposed hideousness of the heavy cap in which the widow laments the "deliverance" of her husband "from the burden of the flesh"? What more revolting than the artificially long faces of the undertaker's men, the drooping "weepers", the carefully-arranged white handkerchiefs, and, until lately, the pall-like funeral cloaks? During the last few years, a great and marked improvement has been made. The plumes, cloaks, and weepers have well-nigh disappeared. The grotesquely ghastly hearse is almost a thing of the past, and the coffin goes forth heaped over with flowers instead of shrouded in the heavy black velvet pall. Men and women, though still wearing black, do not roll themselves up in shapeless garments like sable winding-sheets, as if trying to see how miserable they could make themselves by the imposition of artificial discomforts. Welcome common-sense has driven custom from its throne, and has refused any longer to add these gratuitous annoyances to natural human grief.

In literature and in art, alike, this gloomy fashion of regarding Death has been characteristic of Christianity. Death has been painted as a skeleton grasping a scythe, a grinning skull, a threatening figure with terrible face and uplifted dart, a bony scarecrow shaking an hour-glass--all that could alarm and repel has been gathered round this rightly-named King of Terrors. Milton, who has done so much with his stately rhythm to mould the popular conceptions of modern Christianity, has used all the sinewy strength of his magnificent diction to surround with horror the figure of Death.

The other shape, If shape it might be called, that shape had none Distinguishable in member, joint, or limb, Or substance might be called that shadow seemed, For each seemed either; black it stood as night, Fierce as ten furies, terrible as hell, And shook a dreadful dart; what seemed his head The likeness of a kingly crown had on. Satan was now at hand, and from his seat The monster moving onward came as fast, With horrid strides; hell trembled as he strode.... ... So spoke the grisly terror: and in shape So speaking, and so threatening, grew tenfold More dreadful and deform.... ... but he, my inbred enemy, Forth issued, brandishing his fatal dart, Made to destroy: I fled, and cried out Death! Hell trembled at the hideous name, and sighed From all her caves, and back resounded Death.[1]

That such a view of Death should be taken by the professed followers of a Teacher said to have "brought life and immortality to light" is passing strange. The claim, that as late in the history of the world as a mere eighteen centuries ago the immortality of the Spirit in man was brought to light, is of course transparently absurd, in the face of the overwhelming evidence to the contrary available on all hands. The stately Egyptian Ritual with its Book of the Dead, in which are traced the post-mortem journeys of the Soul, should be enough, if it stood alone, to put out of court for ever so preposterous a claim. Hear the cry of the Soul of the righteous:

O ye, who make the escort of the God, stretch out to me your arms, for I become one of you. (xvii. 22.)

Hail to thee, Osiris, Lord of Light, dwelling in the mighty abode, in the bosom of the absolute darkness. I come to thee, a purified Soul; my two hands are around thee. (xxi. 1.)

I open heaven; I do what was commanded in Memphis. I have knowledge of my heart; I am in possession of my heart, I am in possession of my arms, I am in possession of my legs, at the will of myself. My Soul is not imprisoned in my body at the gates of Amenti. (xxvi. 5, 6.)

Not to multiply to weariness quotations from a book that is wholly composed of the doings and sayings of the disembodied man, let it suffice to give the final judgment on the victorious Soul:

The defunct shall be deified among the Gods in the lower divine region, he shall never be rejected.... He shall drink from the current of the celestial river.... His Soul shall not be imprisoned, since it is a Soul that brings salvation to those near it. The worms shall not devour it. (clxiv. 14-16.)

The general belief in Re-incarnation is enough to prove that the religions of which it formed a central doctrine believed in the survival of the Soul after Death; but one may quote as an example a passage from the Ordinances of Manu, following on a disquisition on metempsychosis, and answering the question of deliverance from rebirths.

Amid all these holy acts, the knowledge of self [should be translated, knowledge of the Self is said (to be) the highest; this indeed is the foremost of all sciences, since from it immortality is obtained.[2]

The testimony of the great Zarathustrean Religion is clear, as is shown by the following, translated from the Avesta, in which, the journey of the Soul after death having been described, the ancient Scripture proceeds:

The soul of the pure man goes the first step and arrives at (the Paradise) Humata; the soul of the pure man takes the second step and arrives at (the Paradise) Hukhta; it goes the third step and arrives at (the Paradise) Hvarst; the soul of the pure man takes the fourth step and arrives at the Eternal Lights.

To it speaks a pure one deceased before, asking it: How art thou, O pure deceased, come away from the fleshy dwellings, from the earthly possessions, from the corporeal world hither to the invisible, from the perishable world hither to the imperishable, as it happened to thee--to whom hail!

Then speaks Ahura-Mazda: Ask not him whom thou asketh, (for) he is come on the fearful, terrible, trembling way, the separation of body and soul.[3]

The Persian Desatir speaks with equal definiteness. This work consists of fifteen books, written by Persian prophets, and was written originally in the Avestaic language; "God" is Ahura-Mazda, or Yazdan:

God selected man from animals to confer on him the soul, which is a substance free, simple, immaterial, non-compounded and non-appetitive. And that becomes an angel by improvement.

By his profound wisdom and most sublime intelligence, he connected the soul with the material body.

If he (man) does good in the material body, and has a good knowledge and religion he is Hartasp....

As soon as he leaves this material body, I (God) take him up to the world of angels, that he may have an interview with the angels, and behold me.

And if he is not Hartasp, but has wisdom and abstains from vice, I will promote him to the rank of angels.

Every person in proportion to his wisdom and piety will find a place in the rank of wise men, among the heavens and stars. And in that region of happiness he will remain for ever.[4]

In China, the immemorial custom of worshipping the Souls of ancestors shows how completely the life of man was regarded as extending beyond the tomb. The Shi King--placed by Mr. James Legge as the most ancient of Chinese classics, containing historical documents ranging from B.C. 2357-627--is full of allusions to these Souls, who with other spiritual beings, watch over the affairs of their descendants and the welfare of the kingdom. Thus Pan-kang, ruling from B.C. 1401-1374, exhorts his subjects:

My object is to support and nourish you all. I think of my ancestors (who are now) the spiritual sovereigns.... Were I to err in my government, and remain long here, my high sovereign (the founder of our dynasty) would send down on me great punishment for my crime, and say, "Why do you oppress my people?" If you, the myriads of the people, do not attend to the perpetuation of your lives, and cherish one mind with me, the One man, in my plans, the former kings will send down on you great punishment for your crime, and say, "Why do you not agree with our young grandson, but go on to forfeit your virtue?" When they punish you from above, you will have no way of escape.... Your ancestors and fathers will (now) cut you off and abandon you, and not save you from death.[5]

Indeed, so practical is this Chinese belief, held to-day as in those long-past ages, that "the change that men call Death" seems to play a very small part in the thoughts and lives of the people of the Flowery Land.

These quotations, which might be multiplied a hundred-fold, may suffice to prove the folly of the idea that immortality came to "light through the gospel". The whole ancient world basked in the full sunshine of belief in the immortality of man, lived in it daily, voiced it in its literature, went with it in calm serenity through the gate of Death.

It remains a problem why Christianity, which vigorously and joyously re-affirmed it, should have growing in its midst the unique terror of Death that has played so large a part in its social life, its literature, and its art. It is not simply the belief in hell that has surrounded the grave with horror, for other Religions have had their hells, and yet their followers have not been harassed by this shadowy Fear. The Chinese, for instance, who take Death as such a light and trivial thing, have a collection of hells quite unique in their varied unpleasantness. Maybe the difference is a question of race rather than of creed; that the vigorous life of the West shrinks from its antithesis, and that its unimaginative common-sense finds a bodiless condition too lacking in solidity of comfort; whereas the more dreamy, mystical East, prone to meditation, and ever seeking to escape from the thraldom of the senses during earthly life, looks on the disembodied state as eminently desirable, and as most conducive to unfettered thought.

Ere passing to the consideration of the history of man in the post-mortem state, it is necessary, however briefly, to state the constitution of man, as viewed by the Esoteric Philosophy, for we must have in mind the constituents of his being ere we can understand their disintegration. Man then consists of

The Immortal Triad:

Amti Buddhi. Manas.

The Perishable Quaternary:

Kana. Prana. Etheric Double. Dense Body.

The dense body is the physical body, the visible, tangible outer form, composed of various tissues. The etheric double is the ethereal counterpart of the body, composed of the physical ethers. Prana is vitality, the integrating energy that co-ordinates the physical molecules and holds them together in a definite organism; it is the life-breath within the organism, the portion of the universal Life-Breath, appropriated by the organism during the span of existence that we speak of as "a life". Kana is the aggregate of appetites, passions, and emotions, common to man and brute. Manas is the Thinker in us, the Intelligence. Buddhi is the vehicle wherein Amti the Spirit, dwells, and in which alone it can manifest.

Now the link between the Immortal Triad and the Perishable Quaternary is Manas, which is dual during earth life, or incarnation, and functions as Higher Manas and Lower Manas. Higher Manas sends out a Ray, Lower Manas, which works in and through the human brain, functioning there as brain-consciousness, as the ratiocinating intelligence. This mingles with Kana, the passional nature, the passions and emotions thus becoming a part of Mind, as defined in Western Psychology. And so we have the link formed between the higher and lower natures in man, this Kana-Manas belonging to the higher by its mosaic, and to the lower by its kamic, elements. As this forms the battleground during life, so does it play an important part in post-mortem existence. We might now classify our seven principles a little differently, having in view this mingling in Kana-Manas of perishable and imperishable elements:

{ Amti Immortal. { Buddhi. { Higher-Manas.

Conditionally Immortal. Kana-Manas.

{ Prana. Mortal. { Etheric Double. { Dense Body.

Some Christian writers have adopted a classification similar to this, declaring Spirit to be inherently immortal, as being Divine; Soul to be conditionally immortal, i.e., capable of winning immortality by uniting itself with Spirit; Body to be inherently mortal. The majority of uninstructed Christians chop man into two, the Body that perishes at Death, and the something--called indifferently Soul or Spirit--that survives Death. This last classification--if classification it may be called--is entirely inadequate, if we are to seek any rational explanation, or even lucid statement, of the phenomena of post-mortem existence. The tripartite view of man's nature gives a more reasonable representation of his constitution, but is inadequate to explain many phenomena. The septenary division alone gives a reasonable theory consistent with the facts we have to deal with, and therefore, though it may seem elaborate, the student will do wisely to make himself familiar with it. If he were studying only the body, and desired to understand its activities, he would have to classify its tissues at far greater length and with far more minuteness than I am using here. He would have to learn the differences between muscular, nervous, glandular, bony, cartilaginous, epithelial, connective, tissues, and all their varieties; and if he rebelled, in his ignorance, against such an elaborate division, it would be explained to him that only by such an analysis of the different components of the body can the varied and complicated phenomena of life-activity be understood. One kind of tissue is wanted for support, another for movement, another for secretion, another for absorption, and so on; and if each kind does not have its own distinctive name, dire confusion and misunderstanding must result, and physical functions remain unintelligible. In the long run time is gained, as well as clearness, by learning a few necessary technical terms, and as clearness is above all things needed in trying to explain and to understand very complicated post-mortem phenomena, I find myself compelled--contrary to my habit in these elementary papers--to resort to these technical names at the outset, for the English language has as yet no equivalents for them, and the use of long descriptive phrases is extremely cumbersome and inconvenient.

For myself, I believe that very much of the antagonism between the adherents of the Esoteric Philosophy and those of Spiritualism has arisen from confusion of terms, and consequent misunderstanding of each others meaning. One eminent Spiritualist lately impatiently said that he did not see the need of exact definition, and that he meant by Spirit all the part of man's nature that survived Death, and was not body. One might as well insist on saying that man's body consists of bone and blood, and asked to define blood, answer: "Oh! I mean everything that is not bone." A clear definition of terms, and a rigid adherence to them when once adopted, will at least enable us all to understand each other, and that is the first step to any fruitful comparison of experiences.

THE FATE OF THE BODY.

The human body is constantly undergoing a process of decay and of reconstruction. First builded into the etheric form in the womb of the mother, it is built up continually by the insetting of fresh materials. With every moment tiny molecules are passing away from it; with every moment tiny molecules are streaming into it. The outgoing stream is scattered over the environment, and helps to rebuild bodies of all kinds in the mineral, vegetable, animal, and human kingdoms, the physical basis of all these being one and the same.

The idea that the human tabernacle is built by countless lives, just in the same way as the rocky crust of our Earth was, has nothing repulsive in it for the true mystic.... Science teaches us that the living as well as the dead organism of both man and animal are swarming with bacteria of a hundred various kinds; that from without we are threatened with the invasion of microbes with every breath we draw, and from within by leucomaines, robes and what not. But Science never yet went so far as to assert with the Occult Doctrine that our bodies, as well as those of animals, plants, and stones, are themselves altogether built up of such beings, which, except larger species, no microscope can detect. So far as regards the purely animal and material portion of man, Science is on its way to discoveries that will go far towards corroborating this theory. Chemistry and physiology are the two great magicians of the future, who are destined to open the eyes of mankind to the great physical truths. With every day, the identity between the animal and physical man, between the plant and man, and even between the reptile and its nest, the rock, and man, is more and more clearly shown. The physical and chemical constituents of all being found to be identical, chemical Science may well say that there is no difference between the matter which composes the ox and that which forms man. But the Occult Doctrine is far more explicit. It says: Not only the chemical compounds are the same, but the same infinitesimal invisible lives compose the atoms of the bodies of the mountain and the daisy, of man and the ant, of the elephant, and of the tree which shelters him from the sun. Each particle--whether you call it organic or inorganic--is a life.[6]

These "lives" which, separate and independent, are the minute vehicles of Prana, aggregated together form the molecules and cells of the physical body, and they stream in and stream out, during all the years of bodily life, thus forming a continual bridge between man and his environment. Controlling these are the "Fiery Lives," the Devourers, which constrain these to their work of building up the cells of the body, so that they work harmoniously and in order, subordinated to the higher manifestation of life in the complex organism called Man. These Fiery Lives on our plane correspond, in this controlling and organising function, with the One Life of the Universe,[7] and when they no longer exercise this function in the human body, the lower lives run rampant, and begin to break down the hitherto definitely organised body. During bodily life they are marshalled as an army; marching in regular order under the command of a general, performing various evolutions, keeping step, moving as a single body. At "Death" they become a disorganised and tumultuous mob, rushing hither and thither, jostling each other, tumbling over each other, with no common object, no generally recognised authority. The body is never more alive than when it is dead; but it is alive in its units, and dead in its totality; alive as a congeries, dead as an organism.

Science regards man as an aggregation of atoms temporarily united by a mysterious force called the life-principle. To the Materialist, the only difference between a living and a dead body is that in the one case that force is active, in the other latent. When it is extinct or entirely latent, the molecules obey a superior attraction, which draws them asunder and scatters them through space. This dispersion must be Death, if it is possible to conceive such a thing as Death, where the very molecules of the dead body manifest an intense vital energy.... Says Eliphas Levi: "Change attests movement, and movement only reveals life. The corpse would not decompose if it were dead; all the molecules which compose it are living and struggle to separate."[8]

Those who have read The Seven Principles of Man,[9] know that the etheric double is the vehicle of Prana, the life-principle, or vitality. Through the etheric double Prana exercises the controlling and co-ordinating force spoken of above, and "Death" takes triumphant possession of the body when the etheric double is finally withdrawn and the delicate cord which unites it with the body is snapped. The process of withdrawal has been watched by clairvoyants, and definitely described. Thus Andrew Jackson Davis, "the Poughkeepsie Seer", describes how he himself watched this escape of the ethereal body, and he states that the magnetic cord did not break for some thirty-six hours after apparent death. Others have described, in similar terms, how they saw a faint violet mist rise from the dying body, gradually condensing into a figure which was the counterpart of the expiring person, and attached to that person by a glistening thread. The snapping of the thread means the breaking of the last magnetic link between the dense body and the remaining principles of the human constitution; the body has dropped away from the man; he is excarnated, disembodied; six principles still remain as his constitution immediately after death, the seventh ody, being left as a cast-off garment.

Death consists, indeed, in a repeated process of unrobing, or unsheathing. The immortal part of man shakes off from itself, one after the other, its outer casings, and--as the snake from its skin, the butterfly from its chrysalis-- emerges from one after another, passing into a higher state of consciousness. Now it is the fact that this escape from the body, and this dwelling of the conscious entity either in the vehicle called the body of desire, the kamic or astral body, or in a yet more ethereal Thought Body, can be effected during earth-life; so that man may become familiar with the excarnated condition, and it may lose for him all the terrors that encircle the unknown. He can know himself as a conscious entity in either of these vehicles, and so prove to his own satisfaction that "life" does not depend on his functioning through the physical body. Why should a man who has thus repeatedly "shed" his lower bodies, and has found the process result, not in unconsciousness, but in a vastly extended freedom and vividness of life--why should he fear the final casting away of his fetters, and the freeing of his Immortal Self from what he realises as the prison of the flesh?

This view of human life is an essential part of the Esoteric Philosophy. Man is primarily divine, a spark of the Divine Life. This living flame, passing out from the Central Fire, weaves for itself coverings within which it dwells, and thus becomes the Triad, the AmtiBuddhi-Manas, the reflection of the Immortal Self. This sends out its Ray, which becomes encased in grosser matter, in the desire body, or koic elements, the passional nature, and in the etheric double and the physical body. The once free immortal Intelligence thus entangled, enswathed, enchained, works heavily and laboriously through the coatings that enwrap it. In its own nature it remains ever the free Bird of Heaven, but its wings are bound to its side by the matter into which it is plunged. When man recognises his own inherent nature, he learns to open his prison doors occasionally and escapes from his encircling gaol; first he learns to identify himself with the Immortal Triad, and rises above the body and its passions into a pure mental and moral life; then he learns that the conquered body cannot hold him prisoner, and he unlocks its door and steps out into the sunshine of his true life. So when Death unlocks the door for him, he knows the country into which he emerges, having trodden its ways at his own will. And at last he grows to recognise that fact of supreme importance, that "Life" has nothing to do with body and with this material plane; that Life is his conscious existence, unbroken, unbreakable, and that the brief interludes in that Life, during which he sojourns on Earth, are but a minute fraction of his conscious existence, and a fraction, moreover, during which he is less alive, because of the heavy coverings which weigh him down. For only during these interludes (save in exceptional cases) may he wholly lose his consciousness of continued life, being surrounded by these coverings which delude him and blind him to the truth of things, making that real which is illusion, and that stable which is transitory. The sunlight ranges over the universe, and at incarnation we step out of it into the twilight of the body, and see but dimly during the period of our incarceration; at Death we step out of the prison again into the sunlight, and are nearer to the reality. Short are the twilight periods, and long the periods of the sunlight; but in our blinded state we call the twilight life, and to us it is the real existence, while we call the sunlight Death, and shiver at the thought of passing into it. Well did Giordano Bruno, one of the greatest teachers of our Philosophy in the Middle Ages, state the truth as to the body and Man. Of the real Man he says:

He will be present in the body in such wise that the best part of himself will be absent from it, and will join himself by an indissoluble sacrament to divine things, in such a way that he will not feel either love or hatred of things mortal. Considering himself as master, and that he ought not to be servant and slave to his body, which he would regard only as the prison which holds his liberty in confinement, the glue which smears his wings, chains which bind fast his hands, stocks which fix his feet, veil which hides his view. Let him not be servant, captive, ensnared, chained, idle, stolid, and blind, for the body which he himself abandons cannot tyrannise over him, so that thus the spirit in a certain degree comes before him as the corporeal world, and matter is subject to the divinity and to nature.[10]

When once we thus come to regard the body, and by conquering it we gain our liberty, Death loses for us all his terrors, and at his touch the body slips from us as a garment, and we stand out from it erect and free.

On the same lines of thought Dr. Franz Hartmann writes:

According to certain views of the West man is a developed ape. According to the views of Indian Sages, which also coincide with those of the Philosophers of past ages and with the teachings of the Christian Mystics, man is a God, who is united during his earthly life, through his own carnal tendencies, to an animal (his animal nature). The God who dwells within him endows man with wisdom. The animal endows him with force. After death, _the God effects his own release from the man_ by departing from the animal body. As man carries within him this divine consciousness, it is his task to battle with his animal inclinations, and to raise himself above them, by the help of the divine principle, a task which the animal cannot achieve, and which therefore is not demanded of it.[11]

The "man", using the word in the sense of personality, as it is used in the latter half of this sentence, is only conditionally immortal; the true man, the evolving God, releases himself, and so much of the personality goes with him as has raised itself into union with the divine.

The body thus left to the rioting of the countless lives--previously held in constraint by Prana, acting through its vehicle the etheric double--begins to decay, that is to break up, and with the disintegration of its cells and molecules, its particles pass away into other combinations.

On our return to Earth we may meet again some of those same countless lives that in a previous incarnation made of our then body their passing dwelling; but all that we are just now concerned with is the breaking up of the body whose life-span is over, and its fate is complete disintegration. To the dense body, then, Death means dissolution as an organism, the loosing of the bonds that united the many into one.

THE FATE OF THE ETHERIC DOUBLE.

The etheric double is the ethereal counterpart of the gross body of man. It is the double that is sometimes seen during life in the neighbourhood of the body, and its absence from the body is generally marked by the heaviness or semi-lethargy of the latter. Acting as the reservoir, or vehicle, of the life-principle during earth-life, its withdrawal from the body is naturally marked by the lowering of all vital functions, even while the cord which unites the two is still unbroken. As has been already said, the snapping of the cord means the death of the body.

When the etheric double finally quits the body, it does not travel to any distance from it. Normally it remains floating over the body, the state of consciousness being dreamy and peaceful, unless tumultuous distress and violent emotion surround the corpse from which it has just issued. And here it may be well to say that during the slow process of dying, while the etheric double is withdrawing from the body, taking with it the higher principles, as after it has withdrawn, extreme quiet and self-control should be observed in the chamber of Death. For during this time the whole life passes swiftly in review before the Ego, the individual, as those have related who have passed in drowning into this unconscious and pulseless state. A Master has written:

At the last moment the whole life is reflected in our memory, and emerges from all the forgotten nooks and corners, picture after picture, one event after another.... The man may often appear dead, yet from the last pulsation, from and between the last throbbing of his heart and the moment when the last spark of animal heat leaves the body, the brain thinks, _and the Ego lives over in those few brief seconds his whole life. Speak in whispers, ye who assist at a deathbed, and find yourselves in the solemn presence of death. Especially have ye to keep quiet just after death has laid her clammy hand upon the body. Speak in whispers, I say, lest ye disturb the quiet ripple of thought, and hinder the busy work of the past, casting its reflection upon the veil of the future._ [12]

This is the time during which the thought-images of the ended earth-life, clustering around their maker, group and interweave themselves into the completed image of that life, and are impressed in their totality on the Astral Light. The dominant tendencies, the strongest thought-habits, assert their pre-eminence, and stamp themselves as the characteristics which will appear as "innate qualities" in the succeeding incarnation. This balancing-up of the life-issues, this reading of the komic records, is too solemn and momentous a thing to be disturbed by the ill-timed wailings of personal relatives and friends.

At the solemn moment of death every man, even when death is sudden, sees the whole of his past life marshalled before him, in its minutest details. For one short instant the personal become one with the individual and all-knowing Ego. But this instant is enough to show to him the whole chain of causes which have been at work during his life. He sees and now understands himself as he is, unadorned by flattery or self-deception. He reads his life, remaining as a spectator, looking down into the arena he is quitting.[13]

This vivid sight is succeeded, in the ordinary person, by the dreamy, peaceful semi-consciousness spoken of above, as the etheric double floats above the body to which it has belonged, now completely separated from it.

Sometimes this double is seen by persons in the house, or in the neighbourhood, when the thought of the dying has been strongly turned to some one left behind, when some anxiety has been in the mind at the last, something left undone which needed doing, or when some local disturbance has shaken the tranquillity of the passing entity. Under these conditions, or others of a similar nature, the double may be seen or heard; when seen, it shows the dreamy, hazy consciousness alluded to, is silent, vague in its aspect, unresponsive.

As the days go on, the five higher principles gradually disengage themselves from the etheric double, and shake this off as they previously shook off the grosser body. They pass on, as a fivefold entity, into a state to be next studied, leaving the etheric double, with the dense body of which it is the counterpart, thus becoming an ethereal corpse, as much as the body had become a dense corpse. This ethereal corpse remains near the dense one, and they disintegrate together; clairvoyants see these ethereal wraiths in churchyards, sometimes showing likeness to the dead dense body, sometimes as violet mists or lights. Such an ethereal corpse has been seen by a friend of my own, passing through the horribly repulsive stages of decomposition, a ghastly vision in face of which clairvoyance was certainly no blessing. The process goes on pari passu, until all but the actual bony skeleton of the dense body is completely disintegrated, and the particles have gone to form other combinations.

One of the great advantages of cremation--apart from all sanitary conditions--lies in the swift restoration to Mother Nature of the physical elements composing the dense and ethereal corpses, brought about by the burning. Instead of slow and gradual decomposition, swift dissociation takes place, and no physical remnants are left, working possible mischief.

The ethereal corpse may to some extent be revivified for a short period after its death. Dr. Hartmann says:

The fresh corpse of a person who has suddenly been killed may be galvanised into a semblance of life by the application of a galvanic battery. Likewise the astral corpse of a person may be brought back into an artificial life by being infused with a part of the life principle of the medium. If that corpse is one of a very intellectual person, it may talk very intellectually; and if it was that of a fool it will talk like a fool.[14]

This mischievous procedure can only be carried out in the neighbourhood of the corpse, and for a very limited time after death, but there are cases on record of such galvanising of the ethereal corpse, performed at the grave of the departed person. Needless to say that such a process belongs distinctly to "Black" Magic, and is wholly evil. Ethereal corpses, like dense ones, if not swiftly destroyed by burning, should be left in the silence and the darkness, a silence and a darkness that it is the worst profanity to break.

KAMALOKA, AND THE FATE OF PRANA AND KAMA.

Loka is a Sanskrit word that may be translated as place, world, land, so that Kamaloka is literally the place or the world of Kana, Kana being the name of that part of the human organism that includes all the passions, desires, and emotions which man has in common with the lower animals.[15] In this division of the universe, the Kamaloka, dwell all the human entities that have shaken off the dense body and its ethereal double, but have not yet disentangled themselves from the passional and emotional nature. Kamaloka has many other tenants, but we are concerned only with the human beings who have lately passed through the gateway of Death, and it is on these that we must concentrate our study.

A momentary digression may be pardoned on the question of the existence of regions in the universe, other than the physical, peopled with intelligent beings. The existence of such regions is postulated by the Esoteric Philosophy, and is known to the Adepts and to very many less highly evolved men and women by personal experience; all that is needed for the study of these regions is the evolution of the faculties latent in every man; a "living" man, in ordinary parlance, can leave his dense and ethereal bodies behind him, and explore these regions without going through Death's gateway. Thus we read in the Theosophist that real knowledge may be acquired by the Spirit in the living man coming into conscious relations with the world of Spirit.

As in the case, say, of an initiated Adept, who brings back upon earth with him the clear and distinct recollection--correct to a detail--of facts gathered, and the information obtained, in the invisible sphere of Realities.[16]

In this way those regions become to him matters of knowledge as definite, as certain, as familiar, as if he should travel to Africa in ordinary fashion, explore its deserts, and return to his own land the richer for the knowledge and experience gained. A seasoned African explorer would care but little for the criticisms passed on his report by persons who had never been thither; he might tell what he saw, describe the animals whose habits he had studied, sketch the country he had traversed, sum up its products and its characteristics. If he was contradicted, laughed at, set right, by untravelled critics, he would be neither ruffled nor distressed, but would merely leave them alone. Ignorance cannot convince knowledge by repeated asseveration of its nescience. The opinion of a hundred persons on a subject on which they are wholly ignorant is of no more weight than the opinion of one such person. Evidence is strengthened by many consenting witnesses, testifying each to his knowledge of a fact, but nothing multiplied a thousand times remains nothing. Strange, indeed, would it be if all the Space around us be empty, mere waste void, and the inhabitants of earth the only forms in which intelligence could clothe itself. As Dr. Huxley said:

Without stepping beyond the analogy of that which is known, it is easy to people the cosmos with entities, in ascending scale, until we reach something practically indistinguishable from omnipotence, omnipresence, and omniscience.[17]

If these entities did not have organs of sense like our own, if their senses responded to vibrations different from those which affect ours, they and we might walk side by side, pass each other, meet each other, pass through each other, and yet be never the wiser as to each other's existence. Mr. Crookes gives us a glimpse of the possibility of such unconscious co-existence of intelligent beings, and but a very slight effort of imagination is needed to realise the conception.

It is not improbable that other sentient beings have organs of sense which do not respond to some or any of the rays to which our eyes are sensitive, but are able to appreciate other vibrations to which we are blind. Such beings would practically be living in a different world to our own. Imagine, for instance, what idea we should form of surrounding objects were we endowed with eyes not sensitive to the ordinary rays of light, but sensitive to the vibrations concerned in electric and magnetic phenomena. Glass and crystal would be among the most opaque of bodies. Metals would be more or less transparent, and a telegraph wire through the air would look like a long narrow hole drilled through an impervious solid body. A dynamo in active work would resemble a conflagration, whilst a permanent magnet would realise the dream of medieval mystics, and become an everlasting lamp with no expenditure of energy or consumption of fuel.[18]

Kamaloka is a region peopled by intelligent and semi-intelligent entities, just as our own is thus peopled; it is crowded, like our world, with many types and forms of living things, as diverse from each other as a blade of grass is different from a tiger, a tiger from a man. It interpenetrates our own world and is interpenetrated by it, but, as the states of matter in the two worlds differ, they co-exist without the knowledge of the intelligent beings in either. Only under abnormal circumstances can consciousness of each other's presence arise among the inhabitants of the two worlds; by certain peculiar training a living human being can come into conscious contact with and control many of the sub-human denizens of Kamaloka; human beings, who have quitted earth and in whom the kamic elements were strong, may very readily be attracted by the kamic elements in embodied men, and by their help become conscious again of the presence of the scenes they had left; and human beings still embodied may set up methods of communication with the disembodied, and may, as said, leave their own bodies for awhile, and become conscious in Kamaloka by the use of faculties through which they have accustomed their consciousness to act. The point which is here to be clearly grasped is the existence of Kamaloka as a definite region, inhabited by a large diversity of entities, among whom are disembodied human beings.

From this necessary digression we return to the particular human being whose fate, as a type, we may be said to be tracing, and of whose dense body and etheric double we have already disposed. Let us contemplate him in the state of very brief duration that follows the shaking off of these two casings. Says H.P. Blavatsky, after quoting from Plutarch a description of the man after death:

Here you have our doctrine, which shows man a septenary during life; a quintile just after death, in Kamaloka.[19]

Prana, the portion of the life-energy appropriated by the man in his embodied state, having lost its vehicle, the ethereal double, which, with the physical body, has slipped away from its controlling energy, must pass back into the great life-reservoir of the universe. As water enclosed in a glass vessel and plunged into a tank mingles with the surrounding water if the vessel be broken, so Prana, as the bodies drop from it, mingles again with the Life Universal. It is only "just after death" that man is a quintile, or fivefold in his constitution, for Prana, as a distinctively human principle, cannot remain appropriated when its vehicle disintegrates.

The man now is clothed, but with the Kana, or body of Kana, the desire body, a body of astral matter, often termed "fluidic," so easily does it, during earth-life, take any form impressed upon it from without or moulded from within. The living man is there, the immortal Triad, still clad in the last of its terrestrial garments, in the subtle, sensitive, responsive form which lent it during embodiment the power to feel, to desire, to enjoy, to suffer, in the physical world.

When the man dies, his three lower principles leave him for ever; i.e., body, life, and the vehicle of the latter, the etheric body, or the double of the living man. And then his four principles--the central or middle principle (the animal soul or Kana, with what it has assimilated from the lower Manas) and the higher Triad--find themselves in Kamaloka.[20]

This desire body undergoes a marked change soon after death. The different densities of the astral matter of which it is composed arrange themselves in a series of shells or envelopes, the densest being outside, shutting the consciousness away from all but very limited contact and expression. The consciousness turns in on itself, if left undisturbed, and prepares itself for the next step onwards, while the desire body gradually disintegrates, shell after shell.

Up to the point of this re-arrangement of the matter of the desire body, the post-mortem experience of all is much the same; it is a "dreamy, peaceful semi-consciousness," as before said, and this, in the happiest cases, passes without vivid awakening into the deeper "pre-devachanic unconsciousness" which ends with the blissful wakening in Devachan, for the period of repose that intervenes between two incarnations. But as, at this point, different possibilities arise, let us trace a normal uninterrupted progression in Kamaloka, up to the threshold of Devachan, and then we can return to consider other classes of circumstances.

If a person has led a pure life, and has steadfastly striven to rise and to identify himself with the higher rather than the lower parts of his nature, after shaking off the dense body and the etheric double, and after Prana has re-mingled with the ocean of Life, and he is clothed only with the Kana, the passional elements in him, being but weak and accustomed to comparatively little activity, will not be able to assert themselves strongly in Kamaloka. Now during earth-life Kana and the Lower Manas are strongly united and interwoven with each other; in the case we are considering Kana is weak, and the Lower Manas has purified Kana to a great extent. The mind, woven with the passions, emotions, and desires, has purified them, and has assimilated their pure part, absorbed it into itself, so that all that is left of Kana is a mere residue, easily to be gotten rid of, from which the Immortal Triad can readily free itself. Slowly this Immortal Triad, the true Man, draws in all his forces; he draws into himself the memories of the earth-life just ended, its loves, its hopes, its aspirations, and prepares to pass out of Kamaloka into the blissful rest of Devachan, the "abode of the Gods", or as some say, "the land of bliss". Kamaloka

Is an astral locality, the Limbus of scholastic theology, the Hades of the ancients, and, strictly speaking, a locality only in a relative sense. It has neither a definite area, nor boundary, but exists within subjective space, i.e., is beyond our sensuous perceptions. Still it exists, and it is there that the astral eidolons of all the beings that have lived, animals included, await their second death. For the animals it comes with the disintegration and the entire fading out of their astral particles to the last. For the human eidolon it begins when the AmtiBuddhi-Mosaic Triad is said to "separate" itself from its lower principles or the reflection of the ex-personality, by falling into the Devachanic state.[21]

This second death is the passage, then, of the Immortal Triad from the Kanalokic sphere, so closely related to the earth sphere, into the higher state of Devachan, of which we must speak later. The type of man we are considering passes through this, in the peaceful dreamy state already described, and, if left undisturbed, will not regain full consciousness until these stages are passed through, and peace gives way to bliss.

But during the whole period that the four principles--the Immortal Triad and Ka--remain in Kamaloka, whether the period be long or short, days or centuries, they are within the reach of the earth-influences. In the case of such a person as we have been describing, an awakening may be caused by the passionate sorrow and desires of friends left on earth, and these violently vibrating kaic elements in the embodied persons may set up vibrations in the desire body of the disembodied, and so reach and rouse the lower Manas, not yet withdrawn to and reunited with its parent, the Spiritual Intelligence. Thus it may be roused from its dreamy state to vivid remembrance of the earth-life so lately left, and may--if any sensitive or medium is concerned, either directly, or indirectly through one of these grieving friends in communication with the medium--use the medium's etheric and dense bodies to speak or write to those left behind. This awakening is often accompanied with acute suffering, and even if this be avoided, the natural process of the Triad freeing itself is rudely disturbed, and the completion of its freedom is delayed. In speaking of this possibility of communication during the period immediately succeeding death and before the freed Man passes on into Devachan, H.P. Blavatsky says:

Whether any living mortal, save a few exceptional cases--when the intensity of the desire in the dying person to return for some purpose forced the higher consciousness _to remain awake, and, therefore, it was really the individuality_, the "Spirit", that communicated--has derived much benefit from the return of the Spirit into the objective plane is another question. The Spirit is dazed after death, and falls very soon into what we call "pre-devachanic unconsciousness."[22]

Intense desire may move the disembodied entity to spontaneously return to the sorrowing ones left behind, but this spontaneous return is rare in the case of persons of the type we are just now considering. If they are left at peace, they will generally sleep themselves quietly into Devachan, and so avoid any struggle or suffering in connection with the second death. On the final escape of the Immortal Triad there is left behind in Kamaloka only the desire body, the "shell" or mere empty phantom, which gradually disintegrates; but it will be better to deal with this in considering the next type, the average man or woman, without marked spirituality of an elevated kind, but also without marked evil tendencies.

When an average man or woman reaches Kamaloka, the spiritual Intelligence is clothed with a desire body, which possesses considerable vigour and vitality; the lower Manas, closely interwoven with Ka during the earth-life just ended, having lived much in the enjoyment of objects of sense and in the pleasures of the emotions, cannot quickly disentangle itself from the web of its own weaving, and return to its Parent Mind, the source of its own being. Hence a considerable delay in the world of transition, in Kamaloka, while the desires wear out and fade away to a point at which they can no longer detain the Soul with their clinging arms.

As said, during the period that the Immortal Triad remain together in Kamaloka, communication between the disembodied entity and the embodied entities on earth is possible. Such communication will generally be welcomed by these disembodied ones, because their desires and emotions still cling to the earth they have left, and the mind has not sufficiently lived on its own plane to find therein full satisfaction and contentment. The lower Manas still yearns towards the gratifications and the vivid highly coloured sensations of earth-life, and can by these yearnings be drawn back to the scenes it has regretfully quitted. Speaking of the possibility of communication between the Ego of the deceased person and a medium, H.P. Blavatsky says in the Theosophist,[23] as from the teachings received by her from the Adept Brothers, that such communication may occur during two intervals:

Interval the first is that period between the physical death and the merging of the spiritual Ego into that state which is known in the Arhat esoteric doctrine as Bar-do. We have translated this as the "gestation" period [pre-devachanic].

Some of the communications made through mediums are from this source, from the disembodied entity, thus drawn back to the earth-sphere--a cruel kindness, delaying its forward evolution and introducing an element of disharmony into what should be an orderly progression. The period in Kamaloka is thus lengthened, the desire body is fed and its hold on the Ego is maintained, and thus is the freedom of the Soul deferred, the immortal Swallow being still held down by the bird-lime of earth.

Persons who have led an evil life, who have gratified and stimulated their animal passions, and have full fed the desire body while they have starved even the lower mind--these remain for long, denizens of Kamaloka, and are filled with yearnings for the earth-life they have left, and for the animal delights that they can no longer--in the absence of the physical body--directly taste. These gather round the medium and the sensitive, endeavouring to utilise them for their own gratification, and these are among the more dangerous of the forces so rashly confronted in their ignorance by the thoughtless and the curious.

Another class of disembodied entities includes those whose lives on earth have been prematurely cut short, by their own act, the act of others, or by accident. Their fate in Kamaloka depends on the conditions which surrounded their outgoings from earthly life, for not all suicides are guilty of felo de se, and the measure of responsibility may vary within very wide limits. The condition of such has been thus described:

Suicides, although not wholly dissevered from their sixth and seventh principles, and quite potent in the seance room, nevertheless to the day when they would have died a natural death, are separated from their higher principles by a gulf. The sixth and seventh principles remain passive and negative, whereas in cases of accidental death the higher and the lower groups actually attract each other. In cases of good and innocent Egos, moreover, the latter gravitates irresistibly toward the sixth and seventh, and thus either slumbers surrounded by happy dreams, or sleeps a dreamless profound sleep until the hour strikes. With a little reflection and an eye to the eternal justice and fitness of things, you will see why. The victim, whether good or bad, is irresponsible for his death. Even if his death were due to some action in a previous life or an antecedent birth, was an act, in short, of the Law of Retribution, still it was not the direct result of an act deliberately committed by the personal _Ego of that life during which he happened to be killed. Had he been allowed to live longer he might have atoned for his antecedent sins still more effectually, and even now, the Ego having been made to pay off the debt of his maker, the personal Ego is free from the blows of retributive justice. The Chohans, who have no hand in the guidance of the living human Ego, protect the helpless victim when it is violently thrust out of its element into a new one, before it is matured and made fit and ready for it._

These, whether suicides or killed by accident, can communicate with those in earth-life, but much to their own injury. As said above, the good and innocent sleep happily till the life-period is over. But where the victim of an accident is depraved and gross, his fate is a sad one.

Unhappy shades, if sinful and sensual, they wander about (not shells, for their connection with their two higher principles is not quite broken) until their death-hour comes. Cut off in the full flush of earthly passions which bind them to familiar scenes, they are enticed by the opportunities which mediums afford to gratify them vicariously. They are the Pishhas, the Incubi and Succubus of medieval times; the demons of thirst, gluttony, lust, and avarice--Elementaries of intensified craft, wickedness, and cruelty; provoking their victims to horrid crimes, and revelling in their commission! They not only ruin their victims, but these psychic vampires, borne along by the torrent of their hellish impulses, at last--at the fixed close of their natural period of life--they are carried out of the earth's aura into regions where for ages they endure exquisite suffering and end with entire destruction.

* * * * *

Now the causes producing the "new being" and determining the nature of Karma are Trishna-thirst, desire for sentient existence-- which is the realisation or consummation of Trishna or that desire. And both of these the medium helps to develop ne plus ultra in an Elementary, be he a suicide or a victim. The rule is that a person who dies a natural death will remain from "a few hours to several short years" within the earth's attraction--i.e., the Kamaloka. But exceptions are the cases of suicides and those who die a violent death in general. Hence, one of such Egos who was destined to live, say, eighty or ninety years--but who either killed himself or was killed by some accident, let us suppose at the age of twenty--would have to pass in the Kamaloka not "a few years," but in his case sixty or seventy years, as an Elementary, or rather an "earth-walker," since he is not, unfortunately for him, even a "Shell." Happy, thrice happy, in comparison, are those disembodied entities who sleep their long slumber and live in dream in the bosom of Space! And woe to those whose Trishna will attract them to mediums, and woe to the latter who tempt them with such an easy Upadanaa. For, in grasping them and satisfying their thirst for life, the medium helps to develop in them--is, in fact, the cause of--a new set of Skandhas, a new body with far worse tendencies and passions than the one they lost. All the future of this new body will be determined thus, not only by the Karma of demerit of the previous set or group, but also by that of the new set of the future being. Were the mediums and spiritualists but to know, as I said, that with every new "angel-guide" they welcome with rapture, they entice the latter into a state which will be productive of untold evils for the new Ego that will be reborn under its nefarious shadow, and that with every seance, especially for materialization, they multiply the causes for misery, causes that will make the unfortunate Ego fail in his spiritual birth, or be reborn into a far worse existence than ever--they would, perhaps, be less lavish in their hospitality._

Premature death brought on by vicious courses, by over-study, or by voluntary sacrifice for some great cause, will bring about delay in Kamaloka, but the state of the disembodied entity will depend on the motive that cut short the life.

There are very few, if any, of the men who indulge in these vices, who feel perfectly sure that such a course of action will lead them eventually to premature death. The "vices" will not escape their punishment; but it is the cause, not the effect, that will be punished, especially an unforeseen, though probable effect. As well call a man a "suicide" who meets his death in a storm at sea, as one who kills himself with "over-study". Water is liable to drown a man, and too much brain work to produce a softening of the brain matter which may carry him away. In such a case no one ought to take a bath for fear of getting faint in it and drowned (for we all know of such cases), nor should a man do his duty, least of all sacrifice himself for even a laudable and highly beneficial cause as many of us do. Motive is everything, and man is punished in a case of direct responsibility, never otherwise. In the victim's case the natural hour of death was anticipated accidentally, while in that of the suicide death is brought on voluntarily and with a full and deliberate knowledge of its immediate consequences. Thus a man who causes his death in a fit of temporary insanity is not a felo de se, to the great grief and often trouble of the Life Insurance Companies. Nor is he left a prey to the temptations of the Kamaloka, but falls asleep like any other victim.

The population of Kamaloka is thus recruited with a peculiarly dangerous element by all the acts of violence, legal and illegal, which wrench the physical body from the soul and send the latter into Kamaloka clad in the desire body, throbbing with pulses of hatred, passion, emotion, palpitating with longings for revenge, with unsatiated lusts. A murderer in the body is not a pleasant member of society, but a murderer suddenly expelled from the body is a far more dangerous entity; society may protect itself against the first, but in its present state of ignorance it is defenceless as against the second.

Finally, the Immortal Triad sets itself free from the desire body, and passes out of Kamaloka; the Higher Manas draws back its Ray, coloured with the life-scenes it has passed through, and carrying with it the experiences gained through the personality it has informed. The labourer is called in from the field, and he returns home bearing his sheaves with him, rich or poor, according to the fruitage of the life. When the Triad has quitted Kamaloka, it passes wholly out of the sphere of earth attractions:

As soon as it has stepped outside the Kamaloka--crossed the "Golden Bridge" leading to the "Seven Golden Mountains"--the Ego can confabulate no more with easy-going mediums.

There are some exceptional possibilities of reaching such an Ego, that will be explained later, but the Ego is out of the reach of the ordinary medium and cannot be recalled into the earth-sphere. But ere we follow the further course of the Triad, we must consider the fate of the now deserted desire body, left as a mere reliquum in Kamaloka.

KAMALOKA. THE SHELLS.

The Shell is the desire body, emptied of the Triad, which has now passed onwards; it is the third of the transitory garments of Soul, cast aside and left in Kamaloka to disintegrate.

When the past earth-life has been noble, or even when it has been of average purity and utility, this Shell retains but little vitality after the passing onwards of the Triad, and rapidly dissolves. Its molecules, however, retain, during this process of disintegration, the impressions made upon them during the earth-life, the tendency to vibrate in response to stimuli constantly experienced during that period. Every student of physiology is familiar with what is termed automatic action, with the tendency of cells to repeat vibrations originally set up by purposive action; thus are formed what we term habits, and we unconsciously repeat motions which at first were done with thought. So strong is this automatism of the body, that, as everyone knows by experience, it is difficult to break off the use of a phrase or of a gesture that has become "habitual."

Now the desire body is during earth-life the recipient of and the respondent to all stimuli from without, and it also continually receives and responds to stimuli from the lower Manas. In it are set up habits, tendencies to repeat automatically familiar vibrations, vibrations of love and desire, vibrations imaging past experiences of all kinds. Just as the hand may repeat a familiar gesture, so may the desire body repeat a familiar feeling or thought. And when the Triad has left it, this automatism remains, and the Shell may thus simulate feelings and thoughts which are empty of all true intelligence and will. Many of the responses to eager enquiries at seances come from such Shells, drawn to the neighbourhood of friends and relatives by the magnetic attractions so long familiar and dear, and automatically responding to the waves of emotion and remembrance, to the impulse of which they had so often answered during the lately closed earth-life. Phrases of affection, moral platitudes, memories of past events, will be all the communications such Shells can make, but these may be literally poured out under favourable conditions under the magnetic stimuli freely applied by the embodied friends and relatives.

In cases where the lower Manas during earth-life has been strongly attached to material objects and to intellectual pursuits directed by a self-seeking motive, the desire body may have acquired a very considerable automatism of an intellectual character, and may give forth responses of considerable intellectual merit. But still the mark of non-originality will be present: the apparent intellectuality will only give out reproductions, and there will be no sign of the new and independent thought which would be the inevitable outcome of a strong intelligence working with originality amid new surroundings. Intellectual sterility brands the great majority of communications from the "spirit world"; reflections of earthly scenes, earthly conditions, earthly arrangements, are plentiful, but we usually seek in vain for strong, new thought, worthy of Intelligences freed from the prison of the flesh. The communications of a loftier kind occasionally granted are, for the most part, from non-human Intelligences, attracted by the pure atmosphere of the medium or sitters.

And there is an ever-present danger in this commerce with the Shells. Just because they are Shells, and nothing more, they answer to the impulses that strike on them from without, and easily become malicious and mischievous, automatically responding to evil vibrations. Thus a medium, or sitters of poor moral character, will impress the Shells that flock around them with impulses of a low order, and any animal desires, petty and foolish thoughts, will set up similar vibrations in the blindly responsive Shells.

Again, the Shell is very easily taken possession of by Elementals, the semi-conscious forces working in the kingdoms of Nature, and may be used by them as a convenient vehicle for many a prank and trick. The etheric double of the medium, and the desire bodies emptied of their immortal Tenants, give the material basis by which Elementals can work many a curious and startling result; and frequenters of seances may be confidently appealed to, and asked whether many of the childish freaks with which they are familiar--pullings of hair, pinchings, slaps, throwing about of objects, piling up of furniture, playing on accordions, &c.--are not more rationally accounted for as the tricky vagaries of sub-human forces, than as the actions of "spirits" who, while in the body, were certainly incapable of such vulgarities.

Let us leave the Shells alone to peacefully dissolve into their elements, and mingle once again in the crucible of Nature. The authors of the Perfect Way put very well the real character of the Shell.

The true "ghost" consists of the exterior and earthly portion of the Soul, that portion which, being weighted with cares, attachments, and memories merely mundane, is detached by the Soul and remains in the astral sphere, an existence more or less definite and personal, and capable of holding, through a sensitive, converse with the living. It is, however, but as a cast-off vestment of the Soul, and is incapable of endurance as ghost. The true Soul and real person, the _anima divina_, parts at death with all those lower affections which would have retained it near its earthly haunts.[24]

If we would find our beloved, it is not among the decaying remnants in Kamaloka that we should seek them. "Why seek ye the living among the dead?"

KAMALOKA. THE ELEMENTARIES.

The word "Elementary" has been so loosely used that it has given rise to a good deal of confusion. It is thus defined by H.P. Blavatsky:

Properly, the disembodied souls of the depraved; these souls having, at some time prior to death, separated from themselves their divine spirits, and so lost their chance for immortality. But at the present stage of learning it has been thought best to apply the term to the spooks or phantoms of disembodied persons, in general to those whose temporary habitation is the Kamaloka.... Once divorced from their higher Triads and their bodies, these souls remain in their Kama envelopes, and are irresistibly drawn to the earth amid elements congenial to their gross natures. Their stay in the Kamaloka varies as to its duration; but ends invariably in disintegration, dissolving like a column of mist, atom by atom, in the surrounding elements.[25]

Students of this series of Manuals know that it is possible for the lower Manas to so entangle itself as to wrench itself away from its source, and this is spoken of in Occultism as "the loss of the Soul."[26] It is, in other words, the loss of the personal self, which has separated itself from its Parent, the Higher Ego, and has thus doomed itself to perish. Such a Soul, having thus separated itself from the Immortal Triad during its earth-life, becomes a true Elementary, after it has quitted the dense and etheric bodies. Then, clad in its desire body, it lives for awhile, for a longer or shorter time according to the vigour of its vitality, a wholly evil thing, dangerous and malignant, seeking to renew its fading vitality by any means laid open to it by the folly or ignorance of still embodied souls. Its ultimate fate is, indeed, destruction, but it may work much evil on its way to its self-chosen doom.

The word Elementary is, however, very often used to describe the lower

Manas in its garment the desire body, not broken away from the higher Principles, but not yet absorbed into its Parent, the Higher Manas. Such Elementaries may be in any stage of progress, harmless or mischievous.

Some writers, again, use Elementary as a synonym for Shell, and so cause increased confusion. The word should at least be restricted to the desire body plus lower Manas, whether that lower Manas be disentangling itself from the elements, in order that it may be re-absorbed into its source, or separated from the Higher Ego, and therefore on the road to destruction.

DEVACHAN.

Among the various conceptions presented by the Esoteric Philosophy, there are few, perhaps, which the Western mind has found more difficulty in grasping than that of Devachan, or the Devaland, or land of the Gods.[27] And one of the chief difficulties has arisen from the free use of the words illusion, dream-state, and other similar terms, as denoting the devachanic consciousness--a general sense of unreality having thus come to pervade the whole conception of Devachan. When the Eastern thinker speaks of the present earthly life as a dream, the solid Western at once puts down the phrases as allegorical and fanciful, for what can be less illusory, he thinks, than this world of buying and selling, of beefsteaks and bottled stout. But when similar terms are applied to a state beyond Death--a state which to him is misty and unreal in his own religion, and which, as he sadly feels, is lacking in all the substantial comforts dear to the family man--then he accepts the words in their most literal and prosaic meaning, and speaks of Devachan as a delusion in his own sense of the word. It may be well, therefore, on the threshold of Devachan to put this question of "illusion" in its true light.

In a deep metaphysical sense all that is conditioned is illusory. All phenomena are literally "appearances", the outer masks in which the One Reality shows itself forth in our changing universe. The more "material" and solid the appearance, the further is it from Reality, and therefore the more illusory it is. What can be a greater fraud than our body, so apparently solid, stable, visible and tangible? It is a constantly changing congeries of minute living particles, an attractive centre into which stream continually myriads of tiny invisibles, that become visible by their aggregation at this centre, and then stream away again, becoming invisible by reason of their minuteness as they separate off from this aggregation. In comparison with this ever-shifting but apparently stable body how much less illusory is the mind, which is able to expose the pretensions of the body and put it in its true light. The mind is constantly imposed on by the senses, and Consciousness, the most real thing in us, is apt to regard itself as the unreal. In truth, it is the thought-world that is the nearest to reality, and things become more and more illusory as they take on more and more of a phenomenal character.

Again, the mind is permanent as compared with the transitory physical world. For the "mind" is only a clumsy name for the living Thinker in us, the true and conscious Entity, the inner Man, "that was, that is, and will be, for whom the hour shall never strike". The less deeply this inner Man is plunged into matter, the less unreal is his life; and when he has shaken off the garments he donned at incarnation, his physical, ethereal, and passional bodies, then he is nearer to the Soul of Things than he was before, and though veils of illusion still dim his vision they are far thinner than those which clouded it when round him was wrapped the garment of the flesh. His freer and less illusory life is that which is without the body, and the disembodied is, comparatively speaking, his normal state. Out of this normal state he plunges into physical life for brief periods in order that he may gain experiences otherwise unattainable, and bring them back to enrich his more abiding condition. As a diver may plunge into the depths of the ocean to seek a pearl, so the Thinker plunges into the depths of the ocean of life to seek the pearl of experience; but he does not stay there long; it is not his own element; he rises up again into his own atmosphere and shakes off from him the heavier element he leaves. And therefore it is truly said of the Soul that has escaped from earth that it has returned to its own place, for its home is the "land of the Gods", and here on earth it is an exile and a prisoner. This view was very clearly put by a Master of Wisdom in a conversation reported by H.P. Blavatsky, and printed under the title "Life and Death."[28] The following extracts state the case:

The Vedatins, acknowledging two kinds of conscious existence, the terrestrial and the spiritual, point only to the latter as an undoubted actuality. As to the terrestrial life, owing to its changeability and shortness, it is nothing but an illusion of our senses. Our life in the spiritual spheres must be thought an actuality because it is there that lives our endless, never-changing immortal. Whereas in every new incarnation it clothes itself in a perfectly different personality, a temporary and short-lived one.... The very essence of all this, that is to say, spirit, force, and matter, has neither end nor beginning, but the shape acquired by this triple unity during its incarnations, their exterior, so to speak, is nothing but a mere illusion of personal conceptions. This is why we call the posthumous life the only reality, and the terrestrial one, including the personality itself, only imaginary._

Why in this case should we call the reality sleep, and the phantasm waking?

This comparison was made by me to facilitate your comprehension. From the standpoint of your terrestrial notions it is perfectly accurate.

Note the words: "From the standpoint of your terrestrial notions," for they are the key to all the phrases used about Devachan as an "illusion." Our gross physical matter is not there; the limitations imposed by it are not there; the mind is in its own realm, where to will is to create, where to think is to see. And so, when the Master was asked: "Would it not be better to say that death is nothing but a birth for a new life, or still better, a going back to eternity?" he answered:

This is how it really is, and I have nothing to say against such a way of putting it. Only with our accepted views of material life the words "live" and "exist" are not applicable to the purely subjective condition after death; and were they employed in our Philosophy without a rigid definition of their meanings, the Vedatins would soon arrive at the ideas which are common in our times among the American Spiritualists, who preach about spirits marrying among themselves and with mortals. As amongst the true, not nominal, Christians so amongst the Vedatins--the life on the other side of the grave is the land where there are no _tears, no sighs, where there is neither marrying nor giving in marriage, and where the just realise their full perfection._

The dread of materialising mental and spiritual conceptions has always been very strong among the Philosophers and oral Teachers of the far East. Their constant effort has been to free the Thinker as far as possible from the bonds of matter even while he is embodied, to open the cage for the Divine Swallow, even though he must return to it for awhile. They are ever seeking "to spiritualise the material", while in the West the continual tendency has been "to materialise the spiritual". So the Indian describes the life of the freed Soul in all the terms that make it least material--illusion, dream, and so on--whereas the Hebrew endeavours to delineate it in terms descriptive of the material luxury and splendour of earth--marriage feast, streets of gold, thrones and crowns of solid metal and precious stones; the Western has followed the materialising conceptions of the Hebrew, and pictures a heaven which is merely a double of earth with earth's sorrows extracted, until we reach the grossest of all, the modern Summerland, with its "spirit-husbands", "spirit-wives", and "spirit-infants" that go to school and college, and grow up into spirit-adults.

In "Notes on Devachan",[29] someone who evidently writes with knowledge remarks of the Devachan

The ?priori _ideas of space and time do not control his perceptions; for he absolutely creates and annihilates them at the same time. Physical existence has its cumulative intensity from infancy to prime, and its diminishing energy from dotage to death; so the dream-life of Devachan is lived correspondentially. Nature cheats no more the Devachanthan she does the living physical man. Nature provides for him far more real bliss and happiness there than she does_ here, _where all the conditions of evil and chance are against him. To call the Devachan existence a "dream" in any other sense than that of a conventional term, is to renounce for ever the knowledge of the Esoteric Doctrine, the sole custodian of truth._

"Dream" only in the sense that it is not of this plane of gross matter, that it belongs not to the physical world.

Let us try and take a general view of the life of the Eternal Pilgrim, the inner Man, the human Soul, during a cycle of incarnation. Before he commences his new pilgrimage--for many pilgrimages lie behind him in the past, during which he gained the powers which enable him to tread the present one--he is a spiritual Being, but one who has already passed out of the passive condition of pure Spirit, and who by previous experience of matter in past ages has evolved intellect, the self-conscious mind. But this evolution by experience is far from being complete, even so far as to make him master of matter; his ignorance leaves him a prey to all the illusions of gross matter, so soon as he comes into contact with it, and he is not fit to be a builder of a universe, being subject to the deceptive visions caused by gross matter--as a child, looking through a piece of blue glass, imagines all the outside world to be blue. The object of a cycle of incarnation is to free him from these illusions, so that when he is surrounded by and working in gross matter he may retain clear vision and not be blinded by illusion. Now the cycle of incarnation is made up of two alternating states: a short one called life on earth, during which the Pilgrim-God is plunged into gross matter, and a comparatively long one, called life in Devachan, during which he is encircled by subtle matter, illusive still, but far less illusive than that of earth. The second state may fairly be called his normal one, as it is of enormous extent as compared with the breaks in it that he spends upon earth; it is comparatively normal also, as being less removed from his essential Divine life; he is less encased in matter, less deluded by its swiftly-changing appearances. Slowly and gradually, by reiterated experiences, gross matter loses its power over him and becomes his servant instead of his tyrant. In the partial freedom of Devachan he assimilates his experiences on earth, still partly dominated by them--at first, indeed, almost completely dominated by them so that the devachanic life is merely a sublimated continuation of the earth-life--but gradually freeing himself more and more as he recognises them as transitory and external, until he can move through any region of our universe with unbroken self-consciousness, a true Lord of Mind, the free and triumphant God. Such is the triumph of the Divine Nature manifested in the flesh, the subduing of every form of matter to be the obedient instrument of Spirit. Thus the Master said:

The spiritual Ego of the man moves in eternity like a pendulum between the hours of life and death, but if these_ _hours, the periods of life terrestrial and life posthumous, are limited in their continuation, and even the very number of such breaks in eternity between sleep and waking, between illusion and reality, have their beginning as well as their end, the spiritual Pilgrim himself is eternal. Therefore the_ hours of his posthumous life, _when unveiled he stands face to face with truth, and the short-lived mirages of his terrestrial existence are far from him, compose or make up, in our ideas, the only reality. Such breaks, in spite of the fact that they are finite, do double service which, perfecting itself constantly, follows without vacillation, though very slowly, the road leading to its last transformation, when, reaching its aim at last, it becomes a Divine Being. They not only contribute to the reaching of this goal, but without these finite breaks Buddhi could never reach it. hes the actor, and its numerous and different incarnations are the actor's parts. I suppose you would not apply to these parts, and so much the less to their costumes, the term of personality. Like an actor the soul is bound to play, during the cycle of births up to the very threshold of PariNirvana, many such parts, which often are disagreeable to it, but like a bee, collecting its honey from every flower, and leaving the rest to feed the worms of the earth, our spiritual individuality, Serious collecting only the nectar of moral qualities and consciousness from every terrestrial personality in which it has to clothe itself, forced by Karma, unites at last all these qualities in one, having then become a perfect being, a Dhyan Chohan._[30]

It is very significant, in this connection, that every devachanic stage is conditioned by the earth-stage that precedes it, and the Man can only assimilate in Devachan the kinds of experience he has been gathering on earth.

A colourless, flavourless personality has a colourless, feeble Devachanic state.[31]

Husband, father, student, patriot, artist, Christian, Buddhist--he must work out the effects of his earth-life in his devachanic life; he cannot eat and assimilate more food than he has gathered; he cannot reap more harvest than he has sown seed. It takes but a moment to cast a seed into a furrow; it takes many a month for that seed to grow into the ripened ear; but according to the kind of the seed is the ear that grows from it, and according to the nature of the brief earth-life is the grain reaped in the field of Aanroo.

There is a change of occupation, a continual change in Devachan, just as much and far more than there is in the life of any man or woman who happens to follow in his or her whole life one sole occupation, whatever it may be, with this difference, that to the Devachan this spiritual occupation is always pleasant and fills his life with rapture. Life in Devachan is the function of the aspirations of earth-life; not the indefinite prolongation of that "single instant," but its infinite developments, the various incidents and events based upon and outflowing from that one "single moment" or moments. The dreams of the objective become the realities of the subjective existence.... The reward provided by Nature for men who are benevolent in a large systematic way, and who have not focussed their affections on an individual or speciality, is that, if pure, they pass the quicker for that through the Lokas into the higher sphere of Tribhuvana, since it is one where the formulation of abstract ideas and the consideration of general principles fill the thought of its occupant.[32]

Into Devachan enters nothing that defileth, for gross matter has been left behind with all its attributes on earth and in Kamaloka. But if the sower has sowed but little seed, the devachanic harvest will be meagre, and the growth of the Soul will be delayed by the paucity of the nutriment on which it has to feed. Hence the enormous importance of the earth-life, _the field of sowing, the place where experience is to be gathered_. It conditions, regulates, limits, the growth of the Soul; it yields the rough ore which the Soul then takes in hand, and works upon during the devachanic stage, smelting it, forging it, tempering it, into the weapons it will take back with it for its next earth-life. The experienced Soul in Devachan will make for itself a splendid instrument for its next earth-life; the inexperienced one will forge a poor blade enough; but in each case the only material available is that brought from earth. In Devachan the Soul, as it were, sifts and sorts out its experiences; it lives a comparatively free life, and gradually gains the power to estimate the earthly experiences at their real value; it works out thoroughly and completely as objective realities all the ideas of which it only conceived the germ on earth. Thus, noble aspiration is a germ which the Soul would work out into a splendid realisation in Devachan, and it would bring back with it to earth for its next incarnation that mental image, to be materialised on earth when opportunity offers and suitable environment presents itself. For the mind sphere is the sphere of creation, and earth only the place for materialising the pre-existent thought. And the soul is as an architect that works out his plans in silence and deep meditation, and then brings them forth into the outer world where his edifice is to be builded; out of the knowledge gained in his past life, the Soul draws his plans for the next, and he returns to earth to put into objective material form the edifices he has planned. This is the description of a Logos in creative activity:

Whilst Brahma formerly, in the beginning of the Kalpas, was meditating on creation, there appeared a creation beginning with ignorance and consisting of darkness.... Brahma beholding that it was defective, designed another; and whilst he thus meditated, the animal creation was manifested.... Beholding this creation also imperfect, Brahma again meditated, and a third creation appeared, abounding with the quality of goodness.[33]

The objective manifestation follows the mental meditation; first idea, then form. Hence it will be seen that the notion current among many Theosophists that Devachan is waste time, is but one of the illusions due to the gross matter that blinds them, and that their impatience of the idea of Devachan arises from the delusion that fussing about in gross matter is the only real activity. Whereas, in truth, all effective action has its source in deep meditation, and out of the Silence comes ever the creative Word. Action on this plane would be less feeble and inefficient if it were the mere blossom of the profound root of meditation, and if the Soul embodied passed oftener out of the body into Devachan during earth-life, there would be less foolish action and consequent waste of time. For Devachan is a state of consciousness, the consciousness of the Soul escaped for awhile from the net of gross matter, and may be entered at any time by one who has learned to withdraw his Soul from the senses as the tortoise withdraws itself within its shell. And then, coming forth once more, action is prompt, direct, purposeful, and the time "wasted" in meditation is more than saved by the directness and strength of the mind-engendered act.

Devachan is the sphere of the mind, as said, it is the land of the Gods, or the Souls. In the before quoted "Notes on Devachan" we read:

There are two fields of causal manifestations: the objective and the subjective. The grosser energies find their outcome in the new personality of each birth in the cycle of evoluting individuality. The moral and spiritual activities find their sphere of effects in Devachan.

As the moral and spiritual activities are the most important, and as on the development of these depends the growth of the true Man, and therefore the accomplishing of "the object of creation, the liberation of Soul", we may begin to understand something of the vast importance of the devachanic state.

THE DEVACHAN

When the Triad has shaken off its last garment, it crosses the threshold of Devachan, and becomes "a Devachan. We have seen that it is in a peaceful dreamy state before this passage out of the earth sphere, the "second death", or "pre-devachanic unconsciousness". This condition is otherwise spoken of as the "gestation" period, because it precedes the birth of the Ego into the devachanic life. Regarded from the earth-sphere the passage is death, while regarded from that of Devachan it is birth. Thus we find in "Notes on Devachan":

As in actual earth-life, so there is for the Ego in Devachan the first flutter of psychic life, the attainment of prime, the gradual exhaustion of force passing into semi-consciousness and lethargy, total oblivion, and--not death but birth, birth into another personality, and the resumption of action which daily begets new congeries of causes that must be worked out in another term of Devachan, and still another physical birth as a new personality. What the lives in Devachan and upon earth shall be respectively in each instance is determined by Karma, and this weary round of birth must be ever and ever run through until the being reaches the end of the seventh Round, or attains in the interim the wisdom of an Arhat, then that of a Buddha, and thus gets relieved for a Round or two.

When the devachanic entity is born into this new sphere it has passed beyond recall to earth. The embodied Soul may rise to it, but it cannot be drawn back to our world. On this a Master has spoken decisively:

To the "Territory of Doubt," there is a variety of spiritual states, but ... as soon as it has stepped outside the Kamaloka, crossed the "Golden Bridge" leading to the "Seven Golden Mountains," the Ego can confabulate no more with easy-going mediums. No Ernest or Joey has ever returned from the Loka, let alone the Arupa Loka, to hold sweet intercourse with men.

In the "Notes on Devachan," again, we read:

Certainly the new Ego, once that it is reborn (in Devachan), retains for a certain time--proportionate to its earth-life--a complete recollection "of his life on earth"; but it can never revisit the Earth from Devachan except in Re-incarnation.

The Devachanis generally spoken of as the Immortal Triad, AmtiBuddhi-Manas, but it is well always to bear in mind that

Atman is no individual property of any man, but is the Divine Essence which has no body, no form, which is imponderable, invisible, and indivisible, that which does not exist and yet is, as the Buddhists say of Nirvana. It only overshadows the mortal; that which enters into him and pervades the whole body being only it's omni-present rays or light, radiated through Buddhi, its vehicle and direct emanation.[34]

Buddhi and Manas united, with this overshadowing of Amti form the Devachan now, as we have seen in studying the Seven Principles, Manas is dual during earth-life, and the Lower Manas is redrawn into the Higher during the Kanalokic interlude. By this reuniting of the Ray and its Source, Manas re-becomes one, and carries the pure and noble experiences of the earth-life into Devachan with it, thus maintaining the past personality as the marked characteristic of the Devachan and it is in this prolongation of the "personal Ego", so to speak, that the "illusion" of the Devachanconsists. Were the mosaic entity free from all illusion, it would see all Egos as its brother-Souls, and looking back over its past would recognise all the varied relationships it had borne to others in many lives, as the actor would remember the many parts he had played with other actors, and would think of each brother actor as a man, and not in the parts he had played as his father, his son, his judge, his murderer, his master, his friend. The deeper human relationship would prevent the brother actors from identifying each other with their parts, and so the perfected spiritual Egos, recognising their deep unity and full brotherhood, would no longer be deluded by the trappings of earthly relationships. But the Devachan at least in the lower stages, is still within the personal boundaries of his past earth-life; he is shut into the relationships of the one incarnation; his paradise is peopled with those he "_loved best with an undying love, that holy feeling that alone survives_," and thus the purified personal Ego is the salient feature, as above said, in the Devachan Again quoting from the "Notes on Devachan":

"_Who goes to Devachan" The personal Ego, of course; but beatified, purified, holy. Every Ego--the combination of the sixth and seventh principles[35]--which after the period of unconscious gestation is reborn into the Devachan, is of necessity as innocent and pure as a new-born babe. The fact of his being reborn at all shows the preponderance of good over evil in his old personality. And while the Karma [of Evil] steps aside for the time being to follow him in his future earth re-incarnation, he brings along with him but the Karma of his good deeds, words and thoughts into this Devachan. "Bad" is a relative term for us--as you were told more than once before--and the Law of Retribution is the only law that never errs. Hence all those who have not slipped down into the mire of unredeemable sin and bestiality go to the Devachan. They will have to pay for their sins, voluntary and involuntary, later on. Meanwhile they are rewarded; receive the effects of the causes produced by them._

Now in some people a sense of repulsion arises at the idea that the ties they form on earth in one life are not to be permanent in eternity. But let us look at the question calmly for a moment. When a mother first clasps her baby-son in her arms, that one relationship seems perfect, and if the child should die, her longing would be to re-possess him as her babe; but as he lives on through youth to manhood the tie changes, and the protective love of the mother and the clinging obedience of the child merge into a different love of friends and comrades, richer than ordinary friendship from the old recollections; yet later, when the mother is aged and the son in the prime of middle life, their positions are reversed and the son protects while the mother depends on him for guidance. Would the relation have been more perfect had it ceased in infancy with only the one tie, or is it not the richer and the sweeter from the different strands of which the tie is woven? And so with Egos; in many lives they may hold to each other many relationships, and finally, standing as Brothers of the Lodge closely knit together, may look back over past lives and see themselves in earth-life related in the many ways possible to human beings, till the cord is woven of every strand of love and duty; would not the final unity be the richer not the poorer for the many-stranded tie? "Finally", I say; but the word is only of this cycle, for what lies beyond, of wider life and less separateness, no mind of man may know. To me it seems that this very variety of experiences makes the tie stronger, not weaker, and that it is a rather thin and poor thing to know oneself and another in only one little aspect of many-sided humanity for endless ages of years; a thousand or so years of one person in one character would, to me, be ample, and I should prefer to know him or her in some new aspect of his nature. But those who object to this view need not feel distressed, for they will enjoy the presence of their beloved in the one personal aspect held by him or her in the one incarnation they are conscious of for as long as the desire for that presence remains. Only let them not desire to impose their own form of bliss on everybody else, nor insist that the kind of happiness which seems to them at this stage the only one desirable and satisfying, must be stereotyped to all eternity, through all the millions of years that lie before us. Nature gives to each in Devachan the satisfaction of all pure desires, and Manas there exercises that faculty of his innate divinity, that he "never wills in vain". Will not this suffice?

But leaving aside disputes as to what may be to us "happiness" in a future separated from our present by millions of years, so that we are no more fitted now to formulate its conditions than is a child, playing with its dolls, to formulate the deeper joys and interests of its maturity, let us understand that, according to the teachings of the Esoteric Philosophy, the Devachanis surrounded by all he loved on earth, with pure affection, and the union being on the plane of the Ego, not on the physical plane, it is free from all the sufferings which would be inevitable were the Devachanpresent in consciousness on the physical plane with all its illusory and transitory joys and sorrows. It is surrounded by its beloved in the higher consciousness, but is not agonised by the knowledge of what they are suffering in the lower consciousness, held in the bonds of the flesh. According to the orthodox Christian view, Death is a separation, and the "spirits of the dead" wait for reunion until those they love also pass through Death's gateway, or-- according to some--until after the judgment-day is over. As against this the Esoteric Philosophy teaches that Death cannot touch the higher consciousness of man, and that it can only separate those who love each other so far as their lower vehicles are concerned; the man living on earth, blinded by matter, feels separated from those who have passed onwards, but the Devachan says H.P. Blavatsky, has a complete conviction "that there is no such thing as Death at all", having left behind it all those vehicles over which Death has power. Therefore, to its less blinded eyes, its beloved are still with it; for it, the veil of matter that separates has been torn away.

A mother dies, leaving behind her little helpless children, whom she adores, perhaps a beloved husband also. We say that her "Spirit" or Ego--that individuality which is now wholly impregnated, for the entire Devachanic period, with the noblest feelings held by its late personality, i.e., love for her children, pity for those who suffer, and so on--is now entirely separated from the "vale of tears," that its future bliss consists in that blessed ignorance of all the woes it left behind ... that the post-mortem spiritual consciousness of the mother will represent to her that she lives surrounded by her children and all those whom she loved; that no gap, no link will be missing to make her disembodied state the most perfect and absolute happiness.[36]

And so again:

As to the ordinary mortal his bliss in Devachan is complete. It is an absolute oblivion of all that gave it pain or sorrow in the past incarnation, and even oblivion of the fact that such things as pain or sorrow exist at all. The Devachanlives its intermediate cycle between two incarnations surrounded by everything it had aspired to in vain, and in the companionship of everything it loved on earth. It has reached the fulfilment of all its soul-yearnings. And thus it lives throughout long centuries an existence of unalloyed happiness, which is the reward for its sufferings in earth-life. In short, it bathes in a sea of uninterrupted felicity spanned only by events of still greater felicity in degree.[37]

When we take the wider sweep in thought demanded by the Esoteric Philosophy, a far more fascinating prospect of persistent love and union between individual Egos rolls itself out before our eyes than was offered to us by the more limited creed of exoteric Christendom. "Mothers love their children with an immortal love," says H.P. Blavatsky, and the reason for this immortality in love is easily grasped when we realise that it is the same Egos that play so many parts in the drama of life, that the experience of each part is recorded in the memory of the Soul, and that between the Souls there is no separation, though during incarnation they may not realise the fact in its fulness and beauty.

We are with those whom we have lost in material form, and far, far nearer to them now than when they were alive. And it is not only in the fancy of the Devachan as some may imagine, but in reality. For pure divine love is not merely the blossom of a human heart, but has its roots in eternity. Spiritual holy love is immortal, and Karma brings sooner or later all those who loved each other with such a spiritual affection to incarnate once more in the same family group.[38]

Love "has its roots in eternity", and those to whom on earth we are strongly drawn are the Egos we have loved in past earth-lives and dwelt with in Devachan; coming back to earth these enduring bonds of love draw us together yet again, and add to the strength and beauty of the tie, and so on and on till all illusions are lived down, and the strong and perfected Egos stand side by side, sharing the experience of their well-nigh illimitable past.

THE RETURN TO EARTH.

At length the causes that carried the Ego into Devachan are exhausted, the experiences gathered have been wholly assimilated, and the Soul begins to feel again the thirst for sentient material life that can be gratified only on the physical plane. The greater the degree of spirituality reached, the purer and loftier the preceding earth-life, the longer the stay in Devachan, the world of spiritual, pure, and lofty effects. [I am here ignoring the special conditions surrounding one who is forcing his own evolution, and has entered on the Path that leads to Adeptship within a very limited number of lives.] The "average time [in Devachan] is from ten to fifteen centuries", H.P. Blavatsky tells us, and the fifteen centuries cycle is the one most plainly marked in history.[39] But in modern life this period has much shortened, in consequence of the greater attraction exercised by physical objects over the heart of man. Further, it must be remembered that the "average time" is not the time spent in Devachan by any person. If one person spends there 1000 years, and another fifty, the "average" is 525. The devachanic period is longer or shorter according to the type of life which preceded it; the more there was of spiritual, intellectual, and emotional activity of a lofty kind, the longer will be the gathering in of the harvest; the more there was of activity directed to selfish gain on earth, the shorter will be the devachanic period.

When the experiences are assimilated, be the time long or short, the Ego is ready to return, and he brings back with him his now increased experience, and any further gains he may have made in Devachan along the lines of abstract thought; for, while in Devachan,

In one sense we can acquire more knowledge; that is, we can develop further any faculty which we loved and strove after during life, provided it is concerned with abstract and ideal things, such as music, painting, poetry, &c.[40]

But the Ego meets, as he crosses the threshold of Devachan on his way outwards--dying out of Devachan to be reborn on earth--he meets in the "atmosphere of the terrestrial plane", the seeds of evil sown in his preceding life on earth. During the devachanic rest he has been free from all pain, all sorrow, but the evil he did in his past has been in a state of suspended animation, not of death. As seeds sown in the autumn for the spring-time lie dormant beneath the surface of the soil, but touched by the soft rain and penetrating warmth of sun begin to swell and the embryo expands and grows, so do the seeds of evil we have sown lie dormant while the Soul takes its rest in Devachan, but shoot out their roots into the new personality which begins to form itself for the incarnation of the returning man. The Ego has to take up the burden of his past, and these germs or seeds, coming over as the harvest of the past life, are the Skandhas, to borrow a convenient word from our Buddhist brethren. They consist of material qualities, sensations, abstract ideas, tendencies of mind, mental powers, and while the pure aroma of these attached itself to the Ego and passed with it into Devachan, all that was gross, base and evil remained in the state of suspended animation spoken of above. These are taken up by the Ego as he passes outwards towards terrestrial life, and are built into the new "man of flesh" which the true man is to inhabit. And so the round of births and deaths goes on, the turning of the Wheel of Life; the treading of the Cycle of Necessity, until the work is done and the building of the Perfect Man is completed.

NIRVANA.

What Devachan is to each earth-life, Nirvana is to the finished cycle of Re-incarnation, but any effective discussion of that glorious state would here be out of place. It is mentioned only to round off the "After" of Death, for no word of man, strictly limited within the narrow bounds of his lower consciousness, may avail to explain what Nirvana is, can do aught save disfigure it in striving to describe. What it is not may be roughly, baldly stated--it is not "annihilation", it is not destruction of consciousness. Mr. A.P. Sinnett has put effectively and briefly the absurdity of many of the ideas current in the West about Nirvana. He has been speaking of absolute consciousness, and proceeds:

We may use such phrases as intellectual counters, but for no ordinary mind--dominated by its physical brain and brain-born intellect--can they have a living signification. All that words can convey is that Nirvana is a sublime state of conscious rest in omniscience. It would be ludicrous, after all that has gone before, to turn to the various discussions which have been carried on by students of exoteric Buddhism as to whether Nirvana does or does not mean annihilation. Worldly similes fall short of indicating the feeling with which the graduates of Esoteric Science regard such a question. Does the last penalty of the law mean the highest honour of the peerage? Is a wooden spoon the emblem of the most illustrious pre-eminence in learning? Such questions as these but faintly symbolise the extravagance of the question whether Nirvana is held by Buddhism to be equivalent to annihilation.[41]

So we learn from the Secret Doctrine that the Nirvana returns to cosmic activity in a new cycle of manifestation, and that

The thread of radiance which is imperishable and dissolves only in Nirvana, re-emerges from it in its integrity on the day when the Great Law calls all things back into action.[42]

COMMUNICATIONS BETWEEN THE EARTH AND OTHER SPHERES.

We are now in position to discriminate between the various kinds of communication possible between those whom we foolishly divide into "dead" and "living," as though the body were the man, or the man could die. "Communications between the embodied and the disembodied" would be a more satisfactory phrase.

First, let us put aside as unsuitable the word Spirit: Spirit does not communicate with Spirit in any way conceivable by us. That highest principle is not yet manifest in the flesh; it remains the hidden fount of all, the eternal Energy, one of the poles of Being in manifestation. The word is loosely used to denote lofty Intelligences, who live and move beyond all conditions of matter imaginable by us, but pure Spirit is at present as inconceivable by us as pure matter. And as in dealing with possible "communications" we have average human beings as recipients, we may as well exclude the word Spirit as much as possible, and so get rid of ambiguity. But in quotations the word often occurs, in deference to the habit of the day, and it then denotes the Ego.

Taking the stages through which the living man passes after "Death", or the shaking off of the body, we can readily classify the communications that may be received, or the appearances that may be seen:

I. While the Soul has shaken off only the dense body, and remains still clothed in the etheric double. This is a brief period only, but during it the disembodied Soul may show itself, clad in this ethereal garment.

For a very short period after death, while the incorporeal principles remain within the sphere of our earth's attraction, it is possible for spirit, under peculiar and favourable conditions, to appear.[43]

It makes no communications during this brief interval, nor while dwelling in this form. Such "ghosts" are silent, dreamy, like sleep-walkers, and indeed they are nothing more than astral sleep-walkers. Equally irresponsive, but capable of expressing a single thought, as of sorrow, anxiety, accident, murder, &c., are apparitions which are merely a thought of the dying, taking shape in the astral world, and carried by the dying person's will to some particular person, with whom the dying intensely longs to communicate. Such a thought, sometimes called an illusory form

May be often thrown into objectivity, as in the case of apparitions after death; but, unless it is projected with the knowledge of (whether latent or potential), or owing to the intensity of the desire to see or appear to some one shooting through, the dying brain, the apparition will be simply automatical; it will not be due to any sympathetic attraction, or to any act of volition, any more than the reflection of a person passing unconsciously near a mirror is due to the desire of the latter.

When the Soul has left the etheric double, shaking it off as it shook off the dense body, the double thus left as a mere empty corpse may be galvanised into an "artificial life"; but fortunately the method of such galvanisation is known to few.

II. While the Soul is in Kamaloka. This period is of very variable duration. The Soul is clad in an astral body, the last but one of its perishable garments, and while thus clad it can utilise the physical bodies of a medium, thus consciously procuring for itself an instrument whereby it can act on the world it has left, and communicate with those living in the body. In this way it may give information as to facts known to itself only, or to itself and another person, in the earth-life just closed; and for as long as it remains within the terrestrial atmosphere such communication is possible. The harm and the peril of such communication has been previously explained, whether the Lower Manas be united with the Divine Triad and so on its way to Devachan, or wrenched from it and on its way to destruction.

III. While the Soul is in Devachan, if an embodied Soul is capable of rising to its sphere, or of coming into rapport with it. To the Devachan as we have seen, the beloved are present in consciousness and full communication, the Egos being in touch with each other, though one is embodied and one is disembodied, but the higher consciousness of the embodied rarely affects the brain. As a matter of fact, all that we know on the physical plane of our friend, while we both are embodied, is the mental image caused by the impression he makes on us. This is, to our consciousness, our friend, and lacks nothing in objectivity. A similar image is present to the consciousness of the Devachan and to him lacks nothing in objectivity. As the physical plane friend is visible to an observer on earth, so is the mental plane friend visible to an observer on that plane. The amount of the friend that ensouls the image is dependent on his own evolution, a highly evolved person being capable of far more communication with a Devachanthan one who is unevolved. Communication when the body is sleeping is easier than when it is awake, and many a vivid "dream" of one on the other side of death is a real interview with him in Kamaloka or in Devachan.

Love beyond the grave, illusion though you may call it,[44] has a magic and divine potency that re-acts on the living. A mother's Ego, filled with love for the imaginary children it sees near itself, living a life of happiness, as real to it as when on earth--that love will always be felt by the children in flesh. It will manifest in their dreams and often in various events--in providential protections and escapes, for love is a strong shield, and is not limited by space or time. As with this Devachanic "mother", so with the rest of human relationships and attachments, save the purely selfish or material.[45]

Remembering that a thought becomes an active entity, capable of working good or evil, we easily see that as embodied Souls can send to those they love helping and protecting forces, so the Devachan thinking of those dear to him, may send out such helpful and protective thoughts, to act as veritable guardian angels round his beloved on earth. But this is a very different thing from the "Spirit" of the mother coming back to earth to be the almost helpless spectator of the child's woes.

The Soul embodied may sometimes escape from its prison of flesh, and come into relations with the Devachan H.P. Blavatsky writes:

Whenever years after the death of a person his spirit is claimed to have "wandered back to earth" to give advice to those it loved, it is always in a subjective vision, in dream or in trance, and in that case it is the Soul of the living seer that is drawn to the disembodied spirit, and not the latter which wanders back to our spheres.[46]

Where the sensitive, or medium, is of a pure and lofty nature, this rising of the freed Ego to the Devachanis practicable, and naturally gives the impression to the sensitive that the departed Ego has come back to him. The Devachanis wrapped in its happy "illusion", and

The Souls, or astral Egos, of pure loving sensitives, labouring under the same delusion, think their loved ones come down to them on earth, while it is their own spirits that are raised towards those in the Devachan.[47]

This attraction can be exercised by the departed Soul from Kamaloka or from Devachan:

A "spirit" or the spiritual Ego, cannot descend to the medium, but it can attract the spirit of the latter to itself, and it can do this only during the two intervals--before and after its "gestation period". Interval the first is that period between the physical death and the merging of the spiritual Ego into that state which is known in the Arhat Esoteric Doctrine as "Bar-do". We have translated this as the "gestation period", and it lasts from a few days to several years, according to the evidence of the Adepts. Interval the second lasts so long as the merits of the old [personal] Ego entitle the being to reap the fruit of its reward in its new regenerated Egoship. It occurs after the gestation period is over, and the new spiritual Ego is reborn--like the fabled Phoenix from its ashes--from the old one. The locality which the former inhabits is called by the northern Buddhist Occultists "Devachan."[48]

So also may the incorporeal principles of pure sensitives be placed en rapport with disembodied Souls, although information thus obtained is not reliable, partly in consequence of the difficulty of transferring to the physical brain the impressions received, and partly from the difficulty of observing accurately, when the seer is untrained.[49]

A pure medium's Ego can be drawn to and made, for an instant, to unite in a magnetic(?) relation with a real disembodied spirit, whereas the soul of an impure medium can only confabulate with the Astral Soul, or Shell, of the deceased. The former possibility explains those extremely rare cases of direct writing in recognised autographs, and of messages from the higher class of disembodied intelligences.

But the confusion in messages thus obtained is considerable, not only from the causes above-named, but also because

Even the best and purest sensitive can at most only be placed at any time en rapport with a particular spiritual entity, and can only know, see, and feel what that particular entity knows, sees, and feels.

Hence much possibility of error if generalisations are indulged in, since each Devachanlives in his own paradise, and there is no "peeping down to earth,"

Nor is there any conscious communication with the flying Souls that come as it were to learn where the Spirits are, what they are doing, and what they think, feel, and see.

What then is being en rapport? It is simply an identity of molecular vibration between the astral part of the incarnated sensitive and the astral part of the dis-incarnated personality. The spirit of the sensitive gets "odylised", so to speak, by the aura of the spirit, whether this be hybernating in the earthly region or dreaming in the Devachan; identity of molecular vibration is established, and for a brief space the sensitive becomes the departed personality, and writes in its handwriting, uses its language, and thinks its thoughts. At such times sensitives may believe that those with whom they are for the moment _en rapport_ descend to earth and communicate with them, whereas, in reality, it is merely their own spirits which, being correctly attuned to those others, are for the time blended with them.[50]

In a special case under examination, H.P. Blavatsky said that the communication might have come from an Elementary, but that it was

Far more likely that the medium's spirit really became _en rapport_ with some spiritual entity in Devachan, the thoughts, knowledge, and sentiments of which formed the substance, while the medium's own personality and pre-existing ideas more or less governed the forms of the communication.[51]

While these communications are not reliable in the facts and opinions stated,

We would remark that it may possibly be that there really is a distinct spiritual entity impressing our correspondent's mind. In other words, there may, for all we know, be some spirit, with whom his spiritual nature becomes habitually, for the time, thoroughly harmonised, and whose thoughts, language, &c., become his for the time, the result being that this spirit seems to communicate with him.... It is possible (though by no means probable) that he habitually passes into a state of rapport with a genuine spirit, and, for the time, is assimilated therewith, thinking (to a great extent if not entirely) the thoughts that spirit would think, writing in its handwriting, &c. But even so, Mr. Terry must not fancy that that spirit is consciously communicating with him, or knows in any way anything of him, or any other person or thing on earth. It is simply that, the rapport established, he, Mr. Terry, becomes for the nonce assimilated with that other personality, and thinks, speaks, and writes as it would have done on earth.... The molecules of his astral nature may from time to time vibrate in perfect unison with those of some spirit of such a person, now in Devachan, and the result may be that he appears to be in communication with that spirit, and to be advised, &c., by him, and clairvoyants may see in the Astral Light a picture of the earth-life form of that spirit.

IV. Communications other than those from disembodied Souls, passing through normal post mortem states.

(a) From Shells. These, while but the cast-off garment of the liberated Soul, retain for some time the impress of their late inhabitant, and reproduce automatically his habits of thought and expression, just as a physical body will automatically repeat habitual gestures. Reflex action is as possible to the desire body as to the physical, but all reflex action is marked by its character of repetition, and absence of all power to initiate movement. It answers to a stimulus with an appearance of purposive action, but it initiates nothing. When people "sit for development", or when at a seance they anxiously hope and wait for messages from departed friends, they supply just the stimulus needed, and obtain the signs of recognition for which they expectantly watch.

(b) From Elementaries. These, possessing the lower capacities of the mind, i.e., all the intellectual faculties that found their expression through the physical brain during life, may produce communications of a highly intellectual character. These, however, are rare, as may be seen from a survey of the messages published as received from "departed Spirits".

(c) From Elementals. These semi-conscious centres of force play a great part at seances, and are mostly the agents who are active in producing physical phenomena. They throw about or carry objects, make noises, ring bells, etc., etc. Sometimes they play pranks with Shells, animating them and representing them to be the spirits of great personalities who have lived on earth, but who have sadly degenerated in the "spirit-world", judging by their effusions. Sometimes, in materialising seances, they busy themselves in throwing pictures from the Astral Light on the fluidic forms produced, so causing them to assume likenesses of various persons. There are also Elementals of a high type who occasionally communicate with very gifted mediums, "Shining Ones" from other spheres.

(d) From Nirmakas. For these communications, as for the two classes next mentioned, the medium must be of a very pure and lofty nature. The Nirmaka is a perfected man, who has cast aside his physical body but retains his other lower principles, and remains in the earth-sphere for the sake of helping forward the evolution of mankind.

Have, out of pity for mankind and those they left on earth, renounced the Nirvanic state. Such an Adept, or Saint, or whatever you may call him, believing it a selfish act to rest in bliss while mankind groans under the burden of misery produced by ignorance, renounces Nirvana and determines to remain invisible in spirit on this earth. They have no material body, as they have left it behind; but otherwise they remain with all their principles even in astral life in our sphere. And such can and do communicate with a few elect ones, only surely not with ordinary mediums.[52]

(e) From Adepts now living on earth. These often communicate with Their disciples, without using the ordinary methods of communication, and when any tie exists, perchance from some past incarnation, between an Adept and a medium, constituting that medium a disciple, a message from the Adept might readily be mistaken for a message from a "Spirit". The receipt of such messages by precipitated writing or spoken words is within the knowledge of some.

(f) From the medium's Higher Ego. Where a pure and earnest man or woman is striving after the light, this upward striving is met by a downward reaching of the higher nature, and light from the higher streams downward, illuminating the lower consciousness. Then the lower mind is, for the time, united with its parent, and transmits as much of its knowledge as it is able to retain.

From this brief sketch it will be seen how varied may be the sources from which communications apparently from "the other side of Death" may be received. As said by H.P. Blavatsky:

The variety of the causes of phenomena is great, and one need be an Adept, and actually look into and examine what transpires, in order to be able to explain in each case what really underlies it.[53]

To complete the statement it may be added that what the average Soul can do when it has passed through the gateway of Death, it can do on this side, and communications may be as readily obtained by writing, in trance, and by the other means of receiving messages, from embodied as from disembodied Souls. If each developed within himself the powers of his own Soul, instead of drifting about aimlessly, or ignorantly plunging into dangerous experiments, knowledge might be safely accumulated and the evolution of the Soul might be accelerated. This one thing is sure: Man is to-day a living Soul, over whom Death has no power, and the key of the prison-house of the body is in his own hands, so that he may learn its use if he will. It is because his true Self, while blinded by the body, has lost touch with other Selves, that Death has been a gulf instead of a gateway between embodied and disembodied Souls.

* * * * *

APPENDIX.

The following passage on the fate of suicides is taken from the Theosophist, September, 1882.

We do not pretend--we are not permitted--to deal exhaustively with the question at present, but we may refer to one of the most important classes of entities, who can participate in objective phenomena, other than Elementaries and Elementals.

This class comprises the Spirits of conscious sane suicides. They are Spirits, and not Shells, because there is not in their cases, at any rate until later, a total and permanent divorce between the fourth and fifth principles on the one hand, and the sixth and seventh on the other. The two duads are divided, they exist apart, but a line of connection still unites them, they may yet reunite, and the sorely threatened personality avert its doom; the fifth principle still holds in its hands the clue by which, traversing the labyrinth of earthly sins and passions, it may regain the sacred penetralia. But for the time, though really a Spirit, and therefore so designated, it is practically not far removed from a Shell.

This class of Spirit can undoubtedly communicate with men, but, as a rule, its members have to pay dearly for exercising the privilege, while it is scarcely possible for them to do otherwise than lower and debase the moral nature of those with and through whom they have much communication. It is merely, broadly speaking, a question of degree; of much or little injury resulting from such communication; the cases in which real, permanent good can arise are too absolutely exceptional to require consideration.

Understand how the case stands. The unhappy being revolting against the trials of life--trials, the results of its own former actions, trials, heaven's merciful medicine for the mentally and spiritually diseased--determines, instead of manfully taking arms against a sea of troubles, to let the curtain drop, and, as it fancies, end them. It destroys the body, but finds itself precisely as much alive mentally as before. It had an appointed life-term determined by an intricate web of prior causes, which its own wilful sudden act cannot shorten. That term must run out its appointed sands. You may smash the lower half of the hand hour-glass, so that the impalpable sand shooting from the upper bell is dissipated by the passing aerial currents as it issues; but that stream will run on, unnoticed though it remain, until the whole store in that upper receptacle is exhausted.

So you may destroy the body, but not the appointed period of sentient existence, foredoomed (because simply the effect of a plexus of causes) to intervene before the dissolution of the personality; this must run on for its appointed period.

This is so in other cases, e.g., those of the victims of accident or violence; they, too, have to complete their life-term, and of these, too, we may speak on another occasion--but here it is sufficient to notice that, whether good or bad, their mental attitude at the time of death alters wholly their subsequent position. They, too, have to wait on within the "Region of Desires" until their wave of life runs on to and reaches its appointed shore, but they wait on, wrapped in dreams soothing and blissful, or the reverse, according to their mental and moral state at, and prior to the fatal hour, but nearly exempt from further material temptations, and, broadly speaking, incapable (except just at the moment of real death) of communicating scio motu with mankind, though not wholly beyond the possible reach of the higher forms of the "Accursed Science," Necromancy. The question is a profoundly abstruse one; it would be impossible to explain within the brief space still remaining to us, how the conditions immediately after death differ so entirely as they do in the case (1) of the man who deliberately lays down (not merely risks) his life from altruistic motives in the hope of saving those of others; and (2) of him who deliberately sacrifices his life from selfish motives, in the hope of escaping trials and troubles which loom before him. Nature or Providence, Fate, or God, being merely a self-adjusting machine, it would at first sight seem as if the results must be identical in both cases. But, machine though it be, we must remember that it is a machine sui generis--

Out of himself he span The eternal web of right and wrong; And ever feels the subtlest thrill, The slenderest thread along.

A machine compared with whose perfect sensitiveness and adjustment the highest human intellect is but a coarse clumsy replica, in petto.

And we must remember that thoughts and motives are material, and at times marvellously potent material, forces, and we may then begin to comprehend why the hero, sacrificing his life on pure altruistic grounds, sinks as his life-blood ebbs away into a sweet dream, wherein

All that he wishes and all that he loves, Come smiling round his sunny way,

only to wake into active or objective consciousness when reborn in the Region of Happiness, while the poor unhappy and misguided mortal who, seeking to elude fate, selfishly loosens the silver string and breaks the golden bowl, finds himself terribly alive and awake, instinct with all the evil cravings and desires that embittered his world-life, without a body in which to gratify these, and capable of only such partial alleviation as is possible by more or less vicarious gratification, and this only at the cost of the ultimate complete rupture with his sixth and seventh principles, and consequent ultimate annihilation after, alas! prolonged periods of suffering.

Let it not be supposed that there is no hope for this class--the sane deliberate suicide. If, bearing steadfastly his cross, he suffers patiently his punishment, striving against carnal appetites still alive in him, in all their intensity, though, of course, each in proportion to the degree to which it had been indulged in earth-life. If, we say, he bears this humbly, never allowing himself to be tempted here or there into unlawful gratifications of unholy desires, then when his fated death-hour strikes, his four higher principles reunite, and, in the final separation that then ensues, it may well be that all may be well with him, and that he passes on to the gestation period and its subsequent developments.

* * * * *

FOOTNOTES:

[Footnote 1: Book ii., from lines 666-789. The whole passage bristles with horrors.]

[Footnote 2: xii. 85. Trans., of Burnell and Hopkins.]

[Footnote 3: From the translation of Dhunjeebhoy Jamsetjee Medhora,

Zoroastrian and some other Ancient Systems, xxvii.]

[Footnote 4: Trans., by Mirza Mohamed Hadi. The Platonist, 306.]

[Footnote 5: The Sacred Books of the East, iii, 109, 110.]

[Footnote 6: Secret Doctrine, vol. i. p. 281.]

[Footnote 7: See ibid., p. 283.]

[Footnote 8: Isis Unveiled, vol. i. p. 480.]

[Footnote 9: Theosophical Manuals, No. 1.]

[Footnote 10: The Heroic Enthusiasts, Trans., by L. Williams. part ii. pp. 22, 23.]

[Footnote 11: Cremation, Theosophical Siftings, vol. iii.]

[Footnote 12: Man: Fragments of Forgotten History, pp. 119, 120.]

[Footnote 13: Key to Theosophy, H.P. Blavatsky, p. 109. Third Edition.]

[Footnote 14: Magic, White and Black, Dr. Franz Hartmann, pp. 109, 110. Third Edition.]

[Footnote 15: See The Seven Principles of Man, pp. 17-21.]

[Footnote 16: Theosophist, March, 1882, p. 158, note.]

[Footnote 17: Essays upon some Controverted Questions, p. 36.]

[Footnote 18: Fortnightly Review, 1892, p. 176.]

[Footnote 19: Key to Theosophy, p. 67.]

[Footnote 20: Ibid., p. 97.]

[Footnote 21: Key to Theosophy, p. 97]

[Footnote 22: Ibid., p. 102.]

[Footnote 23: June, 1882, art. "Seeming Discrepancies."]

[Footnote 24: Pp. 73, 74. Ed. 1887.]

[Footnote 25: Theosophical Glossary, Elementaries.]

[Footnote 26: See The Seven Principles of Man, p.p. 44-46.]

[Footnote 27: The name Sukhat? borrowed from Tibetan Buddhism, is sometimes used instead of that of Devachan. Sukhat? according to Schlagintweit, is "the abode of the blessed, into which ascend those who have accumulated much merit by the practice of virtues", and "involves the deliverance from metempsychosis" (Buddhism in Tibet, p. 99). According to the Prasanga school, the higher Path leads to Nirvana, the lower to Sukhat? But Eitel calls Sukhat?"the Nirvana of the common people, where the saints revel in physical bliss for eons, until they reenter the circle of transmigration" (Sanskrit-Chinese Dictionary). Eitel, however, under "Amitha" states that the "popular mind" regards the "paradise of the West" as "the haven of final redemption from the eddies of transmigration". When used by one of the Teachers of the Esoteric Philosophy it covers the higher Devachanic states, but from all of these the Soul comes back to earth.]

[Footnote 28: See Lucifer, Oct, 1892, Vol. XI. No. 62.]

[Footnote 29: The Path, May, 1890.]

[Footnote 30: Ibid.]

[Footnote 31: "Notes on Devachan," as cited.]

[Footnote 32: "Notes on Devachan," as before. There are a variety of stages in Devachan; the R Loka is an inferior stage, where the Soul is still surrounded by forms. It has escaped from these personalities in the Tribhuvana.]

[Footnote 33: Vishnu Pura, Bk. I. ch. v.]

[Footnote 34: Key to Theosophy, p. 69. Third Edition.]

[Footnote 35: Sixth and seventh in the older nomenclature, fifth and sixth in the later--i.e., Manas and Buddhi.]

[Footnote 36: Key to Theosophy, p. 99. Third Edition.]

[Footnote 37: Ibid., p. 100.]

[Footnote 38: Ibid., p. 101.]

[Footnote 39: See Manual No. 2 Re-incarnation, pp. 60, 61. Third Edition.]

[Footnote 40: Key to Theosophy, p. 105. Third Edition.]

[Footnote 41: Esoteric Buddhism, p. 197. Eighth Edition.]

[Footnote 42: Quoted in the Secret Doctrine, vol. ii. p. 83. The student will do well to read, for a fair presentation of the subject, G.R.S. Mead's "Note on Nirvana" in Lucifer, for March, April, and May, 1893. (Re-printed in Theosophical Siftings).]

[Footnote 43: Theosophist, Sept., 1882, p. 310.]

[Footnote 44: See on "illusion" what was said under the heading "Devachan".]

[Footnote 45: Key to Theosophy, p. 102. Third Edition.]

[Footnote 46: Theosophist, Sept. 1881.]

[Footnote 47: "Notes on Devachan", Path, June, 1890, p. 80.]

[Footnote 48: Theosophist, June, 1882, p. 226.]

[Footnote 49: Summarised from article in Theosophist, Sept., 1882.]

[Footnote 50: Ibid., p. 309.]

[Footnote 51: Ibid., p. 310.]

[Footnote 52: Key to Theosophy, p. 151.]

[Footnote 53: Theosophist, Sept., 1882, p. 310.]

Printed in Great Britain
by Amazon